YOU to the 10th POWER

4 PRACTICAL STEPS TO RADICALLY INCREASE YOUR PERSONAL POWER

DAVID ROSENHAUS

U10

You 10 Publishing

You To The 10th Power
4 Practical Steps To Radically Increase Your Personal Power
David Rosenhaus

ISBN: 978-0-9848642-2-5

www.DavidRosenhaus.com

Design by Dichotomy Design
www.DichotomyDesign.com

Author Photograph: Mariel Pietrykoski.

U^{10}

You 10 Publishing

DEDICATION

To Robin Linke, who showed me that I was using this
process before I ever realized there WAS a process, and who
gently (sometimes) reminds me to follow my own advice on
the all-too-many occasions I forget. Hey, baby.

And to everyone who has ever felt
put off, shit on, pissed off, walked on,
let down, stood up, and knocked down…
and then got right back up again
without even knowing how they did it.

CONTENTS

"It is your decisions
- not your conditions -
that truly shape
the quality of your life."

Anthony Robbins
Entrepreneur, Author
& Peak Performance Strategist

MY STORY

Suicide Solution

Early in 2006 I was one step from killing myself. I had drunk almost an entire bottle of Bailey's Irish Cream and had spent several hours walking around Burbank, CA in the rain, crying my eyes out. I had suffered from depression my entire life and had thought about suicide a million times before. This time I intended to go through with it.

I was on an overpass above the 134 freeway. It wasn't very far above the highway and even in my drunken stupor I knew the fall wouldn't kill me. I was waiting for an 18-wheeler to come so I could drop down in front of it and make sure the deed got done. I had no intention of being one of those attempted suicides that was nothing more than a call for help. I'm also not a big fan of pain, and really didn't want to get mangled but still live.

If I was gonna do it, I was gonna do it right. I envisioned the scene as I waited for the big rig. I would watch it approach, get the timing perfect, and leap. I would hit the truck's grill, and then be trampled by the tires. I figured the initial impact would hurt like hell, but it would be over so quickly it wouldn't matter.

As I ran the scenario over and over in my mind, visualizing in the way we are taught creates our reality, I knew my timing would have to be perfect for it to work. I also knew that my endless crying was impairing my vision. It had been hours, but I couldn't stop. Somewhere in my mind I wondered if there was a limit to how much water the tear ducts could produce.

It also occurred to me that my drunkenness might throw off my timing. Somewhere in my mind I wondered how I could be having these rational thoughts in the midst of my drunken depression.

I eventually realized I wouldn't be able to guarantee my successful demise. Luckily there was a bar just two blocks away. I managed to stop sniveling before going in and after a couple more drinks I finally called my wife to come and pick me up.

This is the point in the story where I'm supposed to say that when I woke up the next morning I had an epiphany and turned my life around. I found the answers, started doing seminars, wrote a best-selling book, and became the next Tony Robbins, Jack Canfield and Oprah Winfrey all rolled into one.

Not quite.

I did find the answers and I do teach seminars and I hope this, my first book, is already a best-seller as you read it now... but it's taken over five years of ups and downs and healing and soul-searching and figuring out who I am and why I'm here.

And I may be the only person ever to *leave* California to find himself.

The Long And Winding Road

I always felt like a loser. I never thought I was good enough, and when I was good at anything I was usually punished for it in some way. If I ever enjoyed myself too much I was usually punished for it in some way. You've probably had that experience, too, right? You laugh too loud or get too excited about something and there's always someone there telling to you stop being loud, stop being rude, stop acting silly, STOP BEING YOU!

So I did. I stopped having fun. I stopped being smart. I stopped asking questions. I stopped being me.

After 40-plus years I finally figured out that the cause of my life-long depression was *because* I wasn't being me. (What the new age gurus call "authentic self".) I thought I was being what I thought everyone wanted me to be. Of course I wasn't doing that either, really. So I wasn't being me, and I wasn't being what everyone wanted me to be. I wasn't even being what I thought I should be which wasn't me or what everyone wanted me to be. HUH???? No wonder I was depressed.

After the non-suicide attempt, I stumbled onto to a spiritual path. Again, it wasn't immediate and I didn't dive right in like so many people do after a life-altering event. I read books by Louise Hay, and Tony Robbins and

Abraham-Hicks and many, many others. They seemed to help for a while and then they didn't. But I was learning little fragments of important knowledge from each of them. I was beginning to learn that the answers are within. I was beginning to learn that I'd always had the answers I needed to be myself, and be powerful, and make a difference in the world by being so.

I learned that I wasn't being the real me, but I had no idea who the real "me" was. What if people didn't like the real me? What if *I* didn't like the real me?

As I started digging in to find out who David really was, the first thing I realized was that I wasn't happy in my marriage. We loved each other very much but there were just too many things that weren't working the way we wanted them too. As we discussed the issues, we discovered that the things the real me wanted were not the same things the real her wanted.

I still didn't really know what I wanted, so I started my life over. I gave my wife everything we owned except my clothes, computer, desk and a couch and moved into a small office space. I took care of my few remaining clients and started being me. I read books, I meditated, I walked.

I found people all over the world through the Internet and learned about different cultures and viewpoints. I tried on different perspectives to see how they fit and didn't care what anyone thought about them.

I expanded my mind, my body and my soul and joined the oneness. That isn't some Eastern-exclusive philosophy that requires wearing monk robes and living on a mountain. It also isn't sitting in meditation 22 hours a day and deluding yourself into thinking that perfection means everyone gets along and there's no pain in the world.

It simply means that we're all cut from the same cloth. We all come from the same stuff. We are all atoms and neurons and electrons and share the same physiological makeup as everything else in the world.

There is a certain inner peace that comes with knowing that underneath it all, we are all part of the same unit that is existence.

In scientific terms, it's realizing that everything which exists is formed from a single ingredient: Energy.

In Western religious terms, it's realizing that God sees every sparrow fall because God IS the sparrow.

In Eastern religious terms, it's realizing we are all one.

In practical terms, it don't mean shit.

Back to Life, Back to Reality

It might seem very romantic (or just plain crazy) to begin living like a monk, but unless you actually *are* a monk, it's not a very practical lifestyle. My room was a 10' x 10' office and I took sponge baths from the sink in the men's room. I kept a very low profile at night because it was illegal for me to live there. I had a microwave, but no refrigerator and had to go to the store several times per day if I wanted to eat. I had no car, and was only making about $200 per month.

And I was happier than I'd been my entire life. Unfortunately, I knew I couldn't continue living like that forever.

I spent a lot of years suffering from either stress or depression or both. My experience never fit the mold the "experts" tried to place me in. Their definitions just didn't add up for me. So with all due respect to the medical and psychiatric communities, for the purposes of this book the following definitions apply:

STRESS happens when our perception of something is out of alignment with what we want.

DEPRESSION happens when our actions are out of alignment with who we are.

While personal power (empowerment) is more closely related to an emotion, or state of being, than any action, we are physical beings in a physical world. I know, I know… As a "new-ager" I'm supposed to say that we are spiritual beings in a physical world. As true as that may be, when we start vibrating in the lower registers of fear and stress and anger and depression, that doesn't seem to matter much, does it? When we are in a state of stress, depression, fear, despair, helplessness, hopelessness and haplessness, we need practical, physical, DOABLE steps to get us back in touch with our personal power.

If you're anything like me, you've tried to transcend the damn mind and find a higher vibrating, spiritual place from which to exist. Then some idiot dumps his crap on you and you're back down to Earth ready to pound the jerk into the lower vibrating pavement.

Through much trial and error, I've discovered that the spiritual and physical worlds don't have to be separate. We can recognize the divine within at the same we are in a state of depression or anger. One does not shut out the other, and both can exist in you at the same time.

Even better, once you've had the EXPERIENCE of both at the same time, you will find it much easier to choose the vibration you want to be in and HOW you are being while in it. I still experience mild depression once in a while, but because of the tools you are about to learn, I only stay there as long as I choose to.

Because I no longer get LOST in it, I can honor the feeling fully before leaving it. Most of the time we run from, hide from, or attempt to suppress our "negative" emotions. As any half-baked shrink can tell you, it is important to actually DEAL with our emotions, not hide or bury them.

The tools in this book will help you deal with your emotions in a practical way that doesn't require years on a therapist's couch. I'm not knocking therapists. I've had some very good ones who helped me a lot. We all need help sometimes. The purpose of this book is to help you help yourself with tools you can use on a daily basis whether you are in the midst of crisis, preparing for a stressful situation, or after dealing with a crap-filled day.

EASY AS P.I.E.
Perception Is Everything

We have many different filters that affect our perception of every situation. Before we get to the 4 Steps to Radically Increase Your Personal Power, I want to walk you through several layers of how we look at things, and then play with some alternative ways of seeing them.

We often don't even realize that alternatives exist, forget about seeing what they are and choosing. Let's take the alarm clock for example. Every day the alarm clock rings. Some days it sounds like a death toll that causes us to hide under the covers and pray for it to be any day other than today. Other days it's a starting gun that launches us into the race with excitement and determination.

The alarm itself never changes. It's the same sound at the same volume at the same time. Aren't we also the same every day? In the forty (ahem, mumble, cough) years I've been around, I'm pretty sure I'm pretty much the same person every day. So why does the consistent sound of the alarm evoke so many inconsistent responses?

It's all about perception. Perception is how we filter things. Some people tend to see life through "rose colored glasses". Other people can find the dark cloud inside every silver lining.

When police interview eyewitnesses of a crime, they get completely different accounts of the situation from each witness. This happens because each person views each event through their own filters. Even though they are viewing the exact same thing, they actually see it differently.

Just like the sound of the alarm, each of us has the capacity to see (hear, smell, taste, feel) the same thing in different ways depending on our perception of the moment. If we love our job, we will usually welcome the alarm. If we don't, we can dread it. But then again, even someone who loves their job can dread the alarm on the day of performance reviews or a visit from the district manager.

I made a little visual game using pictures to really illustrate how a simple change in perception can change our understanding of a situation. In this game, you are placed too close to an object to understand what you are looking at. It is only when you step back that you are able to see the whole picture. Go to *www.DavidRosenhaus.com/You10/games* and see how you do.[1]

Once you realize how every situation looks different from a different perspective, you will hopefully not allow the events in your life to stress you out so quickly. You can choose your perspective in any situation. If you don't like the feeling you have, change your perspective.

---

[1] The game is a learning tool. The idea isn't to get it "right". The idea is to learn to recognize how your perception of something affects your ability to understand it, and then apply that experience to your life.

That guy who cuts you off on the highway may be in a hurry because he will lose his job if he's late one more time. He may have a medical emergency. Yes, he may just be a jerk, but he may be a jerk because that's how his parents raised him. He may not know any other way to behave.

I'm not condoning or excusing dumb-ass behavior. I'm only suggesting you recognize that you don't really know the whole story. If your anger, hurt, or resentment is based on your judgment of another person, then you are almost guaranteed to be wrong. *(See Hmmmm... I Could Be Wrong on page 119.)*

Waking up to the Truth that you create every aspect of your life is not easy. It goes against everything most of us have been taught since the day we were born. Our society is built on the idea that other people run things and we have to obey. Whether it's the government, parents, bosses, teachers, preachers or God, it has been drilled into us that we must follow the rules placed on us. When our leaders fail, we look for new ones to follow. When our gods fall, we replace them with others.

The idea that we, each of us individually, are responsible for our lives is too much for most people. Even though it has been part of the world's spiritual teachings for thousands of years, very few people are actually willing to carry the burden of personal responsibility.

Changing Your Perception

Thousands of people commute to work every morning. They drive the same routes as each other, on the same roads, in the same weather conditions at the same time. Some get to work stressed and miserable, while others arrive upbeat and ready to be productive. For some, the drive is depressing and for others it's invigorating.

So what's the difference? Is it attitude? Well, yes, but it's not always easy to just change your attitude on a dime. Is it negative thinking? Yes, but thinking positive seems to be downright impossible sometimes, especially when you're in the thick of the drama.

The problem is that while the answer is usually pretty simple, the PROCESS takes WORK! The hardest part of the work is the honesty it takes in recognizing what the real issues are, what the truth is, what YOUR truth is. Once you identify the truth, there is another issue: What do you do about it?

There is profound truth in the saying "the only constant is change". Things go much smoother when we embrace the changes that happen. For real empowerment though, you must be the one who makes the change instead of waiting for things to happen to you.

REAL LIFE EXAMPLE

There's a saying among rip-off artists that the "mark" wants to be fleeced. In many ways I think that's true. When I got caught up in a real estate scam, I saw the warning signs and ignored them. I wanted so much to believe I could make a large chunk of money quickly and easily that I allowed someone to use my name and my credit without fully checking them out. I can blame the scam artist all I want, but it was my choice to ignore the signs. It was my choice to not do the proper due diligence. It was my choice to ignore my wife's protests and warnings and sign papers that ultimately put me into foreclosure on a property I hadn't even seen.

When I went to the police they said I was involved in the fraud, not a victim of it. I went to the Sherriff and I went to the FBI. None of them did anything about it, even though I'd compiled evidence that it wasn't the first time this man had perpetrated this kind of fraud and was breaking several other laws as well.

I could rant and rail about the unfairness of it all, but it was my own choices that put me in that position. I could also beat myself up for being such an idiot.

But let's look at it from a different perspective. I could have spent tens of thousands of dollars on a college education and never learned the valuable lessons I learned from this one experience. I learned firsthand about how the real estate market really works. I learned firsthand how certain lawyers care more about their own ego than helping their clients. I learned that there are honest and affordable services out there for people who need help. And I learned, once again, that I can survive even when I screw up.

All that hands-on learning and experience in less than a year is pretty cool when you get right down to it.

There will always be people who try to disempower us. There will also always be people who try to empower us. When it gets down to it, though, all those people can do is offer you the opportunity. It is your choice which way you want to go.

I think it's safe to say everyone has, at one time or another, felt like a victim. Many people are actually very comfortable being victimized. As a victim we can blame our problems on someone else.

Ultimately it is only up to you to use the tools in this book or not.

The process gets quicker and easier every time you do it. At first, it may not be easy to do in the moment of stress, so try to practice in a safe space. You do this by visualizing a situation where you are under attack, or uncomfortable, or feeling disempowered, then in your mind's eye, see yourself using the process. The more you practice while in a safe space, more prepared you'll be for the real thing. Just make sure you really do put it into practice. If you don't practically apply these techniques, they will do you no good.

You may find that you're nervous about doing it for real. That's cool. It's a new thing, and you don't know how people will react or judge you.

"The ones who are crazy enough to think that they can change the world, are the ones who do."
~ *Steve Jobs*

Just remember that I'm not asking you to change the world. Only yourself. For the better.

Judgmental Thoughts

We are always making judgments. Think about it. Almost every time we use an adjective we are being judgmental. The judgment may not be in the word itself, but in our thoughts (however subtle) behind the words.

What do you really mean by the words that come into your mind or out of your mouth? We might describe someone as being short, tall, fat, or thin. By themselves, those seem like fairly innocuous words. But if you think of yourself as tall, you might be looking down on a shorter person not only physically, but judgmentally as well. You might feel just a hint of superiority. If you look deeper you'll realize that you cannot be superior unless the other person is inferior. You've judged them even if you didn't mean to.

When you describe someone as "smart", are you really judging them as being "stuck up"? Or are you judging yourself as being "stupid"?

This isn't about coming down on you and making you feel guilty for being judgmental. In other words, don't judge yourself for judging. Our judgments are a very important part of our thinking and learning process. The mistake embedded in the way we've learned to judge is that we use our judgment as a moral imperative instead of a guideline from which we can make informed decisions of what is effective for us.

Again I ask you to pay attention to your deeper feelings. Do you look down on someone who disagrees with you in any way?

If you look at sports fanatics you'll see a beautifully exaggerated example of what I'm talking about. If you don't like the same team as someone else, they will think of you as a loser, traitor, idiot, communist, miscreant, radical, law-breaking, douche-bag.

An example from my own personal experience is being called an idiot for not liking strawberry ice cream. Really?

I'm an IDIOT because I don't like the same flavor of food you do? I have no doubt that if I'd questioned the person quietly (instead of telling him to "F"-off) we would have arrived at the insight that he just couldn't understand how someone didn't love a flavor that he found so delectable.

I encourage you to really pay attention to the emotional meanings of the words you think and speak.

Mastering The Basics

We live in a very fast-paced world. We've been able to get so much so fast so often we can't stand it when we don't have what we want RIGHT NOW!

I encourage you to not get frustrated if you don't "get it" the first time you use the tools in this book. Use it like a reference book and allow yourself the luxury of going over what you learn here again and again until you master the basics. If you fully understand the lessons and techniques and are able to apply them immediately with great success, that is wonderful. But please don't get discouraged if your new life introduces you to newer more challenging situations and you find you need to go "back to basics" to work through them.

REAL LIFE EXAMPLE

When I first started working with computers, I learned very quickly. I'd never worked on a computer before and still went from new hire to manager in six months. The very first thing I learned is that restarting the computer clears its memory and resets the system which removes most of the problems. As I learned more and more I was able to diagnose intricate problems with the software and hardware. I could troubleshoot issues that left most of the other people in the department dumbfounded. One day a computer was giving one of the guys trouble. He couldn't figure it out so he called me over. We spent the next three hours troubleshooting and diagnosing and speculating and testing to find where the problem was and how to fix it.

Our newest hire had been there about a week and was standing close watching and learning. As our frustration built, he quietly asked if we had restarted the computer. I can't remember if I literally slapped my forehead, but it was a great reminder that no matter how advanced you may be, all that information is founded on the basics. We restarted the computer and the problem, although never identified, was gone.

Many of the techniques in this book took me years and years of reliving the same situations over and over in the same way before mastering them. And I still fall back into old habits sometimes.

We are all human and our primal instincts run deep. Survival (the fight or flight instinct), is a part of who we are, and always will be, no matter how "civilized" or "advanced" we think we are. When emotions run high because of fear, desire, lust, hunger, or any other primal feelings, they can overtake us regardless of how many years we've had of successfully applying these techniques.

So don't beat yourself up if you aren't "cured" after reading this book once, or even several times. Just go back to step one and read and practice the techniques again. Rinse and repeat.

What Power Is

Power can be problematic. If you've ever seen the sitcom Home Improvement, you've seen that too much power is a dangerous thing (much to our comic delight). If you've seen the effects of the atomic bomb or Hitler's attempt at world domination you've seen that too much power is a dangerous thing (not so funny).

Everything has some degree of power and that power can either hurt or heal. A knife can be used to save a life or to take one. The same electricity that lights and warms your home can also fry you to death. A brick can be used to build or to bludgeon.

We all look at power differently. There is a book called 48 Laws of Power by Robert Greene that discusses the different uses of social and political power throughout history and how it is applied. I found it to be a very interesting read about the psychology of people who try to control others. I learned about many of the ways I'd been manipulated in the past and found the book to be a great tool in self-defense that has prepared me for future instances where people might try to control me. I recommended it to a friend of mine who refused to even consider reading it. She said she didn't want that kind of negativity in her life. Our differences in opinion were based on our differences in perception. It's probably one of the reasons that many women will take a self-defense class but not a martial arts class. They are basically the same thing, but martial arts is often seen to be about fighting while self-defense is seen to be about protection. Is there really a difference? Not if you understand that no matter what you call it, it is only a tool. The "good" or "bad" of it is based on how it is used.

There is a great line from the Spiderman movie I love to quote often: "With great power, comes great responsibility." We humans like to use our power to control others. We've all done it. Some people use brute force, some use persuasive words, and some use guilt. Children learn very quickly that being persistent is a very powerful tool against a parent to get their way. Why? Why? Why? Why? Why? Why? Why? Why? Why? Why? Why? Why? Why? Why? Why? Why? Why? Why? Why? Why? Why? Why? Why? (You probably used that one yourself when you were a kid, right?)

All of that refers to the APPLICATION of power. But what is power?

Power is the "*ability* to do or act".

Regardless of whether you *choose* to take action or not, you already have all the power you need inside you. The problem is that because of the way we are raised and the things we are taught, we often feel as though we have no power. Our parents have been telling us NO from the moment we could move. We have rules and regulations imposed on us in every area of our lives. Literally every person we meet, every place we go, and everything we do imposes rules, regulations, guidelines and limitations on us. In other words, we live in a society where we are taught to be powerless. We are literally trained from birth to follow. The majority of people who attempt to lead, break rules, or create anything that doesn't fit within the comfort zone of what is currently seen as acceptable are met with ridicule, resistance, and often hostility. Even if they can ignore those who would keep them in a box they will still fail more often than not. If they succeed, they are often treated with the resentment of "who do they think they are".

Very few people have the wherewithal to ignore the painful feelings of failure. We are supported in our failure, but are rarely supported in our success. The most successful people in the world fail every day. They just don't stop at failure. They keep taking action until they succeed. They refuse to be beaten down by anyone or anything, including themselves. They have the persistence of a child asking "why?"

I started writing this book (in one form or another) over a dozen times and failed every time. Until now. You're reading the book, so obviously I succeeded. Finally! Whew!

If you don't quit, you don't fail. It's that simple. It may take time. It will most likely be challenging, but if you don't quit, you don't fail.

If accepting that you have all the power you ever wanted seems crazy or just plain scary, it doesn't have to be. Just take a deep breath and read slowly. My intent is to create a foundation for your understanding of where we're going with this book. Personally I usually learn best when I know where I'm going first, then learn how to get there. Sort of like building a house. You could certainly start by laying bricks, but if you don't have a blueprint... a very clear map of what you're building... you'll end up with a very poorly structured house where the roof and foundation are likely to collapse at the same time.

So let's start at the end: You are a divine being. You are one with the Universe. I am you, you are me, we are all one.

This is not a new concept. It's been taught for thousands and thousands of years in different cultures around the globe. The problem is that there's no practical reference point for it for most people. It's a fairy tale. It's some sort of spiritual or religious high-brow concept that doesn't apply to our physical life here in the real world. In a world where the vast majority of people are either struggling to maintain a minimally comfortable lifestyle, or literally fighting for survival, the idea that "we are one" is basically irrelevant. At best it's a romantic notion and at worst it's religious horse-hockey.

I try to approach all my concepts from a practical viewpoint, and I had a very hard time accepting not only the idea of oneness, but its relevance to self-empowerment. The point is that I understand your skepticism, so just bear with me while I flesh this out.

Most people struggle with applying spiritual teachings to real-world situations. We question where god is when we lose our job or a loved one. We see wars and murders and starvation all over the world and wonder how anything we've been taught about the way the Universe works on a spiritual level could possibly make sense.

Here's the deal…. leaders (of any group: religious, ethnic, cultural) are very much caught up in the power struggle of whatever group they belong to. Believe me when I say it's not a knock against any individual of any group. Like most man-made institutions, religious groups are subject to the human foibles of greed and power. More murders have been committed in the name of god and religion than every other motive combined. At its highest vibration, religious groups are formed to create a community of like-minded people. The problem with any community is that it needs a leader. That leader is human and the power of being a leader of others is very intoxicating. (Note the root of that word: toxic.)

Most people are afraid of power, especially their own, and gladly give their personal power to the one who assumes the leadership role. It's much easier to be part of the rank and file, so we abdicate our responsibility.

There are a multitude of reasons for this, but I think the most harmful reason is associated with worry about how other people think of us. We are often taught that stepping outside the 'norm' or being original will result in some kind of negative reaction. Let me tell you... it will. There will ALWAYS be someone who doesn't like what you do. Even if you follow every rule and regulation. There is always someone looking to judge and criticize. So if your fear is about being judged, then you have nothing to worry about. It's already happening. If they are going to judge you anyway, you might as well be judged for doing something that you like and want and feels good to you, instead of being judged for following someone else's rules.

If you want to fully understand, appreciate, and utilize your personal power, you must stop thinking that your power has anything to do with what anyone else thinks, feels or accomplishes. Say it with me: "My dearest Parent, Spouse, Boss, Friend, Fellow Human Being... I love you.

I respect your opinions, but they are YOURS and they are OPINIONS. I am awesome exactly as I am, warts and all. Thank you."

Once you realize and accept that there will always be people judging you no matter what, you are free to be the YOU you've always wanted to be!

The Dimmer Switch

If you think about electricity and how we use it, you will understand your own personal power a little better. The biggest difference between our power and the power of electricity is that we don't need machines and generators and wires to create or use our power. It is always there. It is always available. Like the electricity in our homes, we filter and funnel the power only to do what we need or want. A lamp doesn't use a whole lot of electricity but it is still plugged in to the same power source as the air conditioner.

Each appliance filters the energy so that it doesn't overload itself. You can put a 15 watt bulb or a 60 watt bulb or a 150 bulb into the same lamp. The lamp always has access to the full amount of electricity (power) it can handle, but each bulb only generates the amount of light it is limited to.

We humans also have access to the full amount of Universal power, but we have told ourselves there is a finite amount of light we can shine. We've been told by our parents, teachers and others that we are dim and should remain dim. When we shine too brightly (i.e. are too happy, too loud, too successful, etc) it hurts their eyes (ears, hearts, egos). So we tone it down. We learn from a very young age to use the dimmer switch.

There are a multitude of reasons we are taught to (and choose to) dim it down, but ultimately it comes down to the desire for acceptance. Our parents want to be accepted by society and they want us to be accepted. The general rule of thumb is that to be accepted one must conform.

Some people's light shines so brightly that no amount of external pressure can contain them. Albert Einstein, Eleanor Roosevelt, Janice Joplin, Jim Morrison, Gandhi, Jesus, Susan B. Anthony, and Joan of Arc were all people who broke the rules. They rejected the judgments and attempts at limitation from others and paved their own way in the world. All were vilified and all were idolized. Ultimately, any person who breaks the rules in the name of freedom changes the world for the better.

Yes, it is risky to suddenly start exercising your personal power. The people who expect you to always do what they want might be very surprised the first time you say no to a request or suggest a way of doing something that is more suited to your desire than theirs. They might be hurt and shocked when you ask for what you want for once. They may fight you and try to get you to act "normal".

That's ok. It might be uncomfortable for you, too, at first. We haven't been trained to think or act for ourselves. We've been trained to follow orders.

For those of us who rarely, if ever, stood in our power before now, we really need to re-train ourselves from the ground up. I can remember many specific situations when I was younger and stood fully in my joy or fear or desire and been shunned, laughed at, ridiculed, and accused of all manner of impropriety.

As a quick side note, part of being fully empowered is expressing your full Truth in each moment. That means if your feelings are hurt, you admit it. If you are happy, you show it.

It means if you are angry, you fully express that anger in a safe and healthy way. I'm not suggesting throwing a temper tantrum and acting like a 5-year-old every time something goes wrong. As an empowered adult you choose how you express your emotions.

Children don't have the tools and experience to express themselves in a healthy manner. They get upset or hurt and they react in a physical way immediately. Some lash out with violence and some withdraw into silence. This is because they don't know how to process the emotions and communicate what they feel. In other words, they go directly into fight or flight mode.

Unfortunately, few of us are taught healthy ways of expressing ourselves. We are only told to STOP IT! This isn't an assault on parents. A person cannot teach what they never learned. Now we are finally learning!

I invite you now to turn up your light and shine as bright as you can!

Resistance Is Futile

In Byron Katie's The Work, the first question is, "Is it true?" Nobody has that answer but you. For most of us, in the beginning of learning that the truth lies within, we suddenly get some exaggerated version of Jack Nicholson shouting in our head, "You can't HANDLE the truth!" We don't realize that the voice we hear isn't ours. It is the voice of our parents, teachers, friends and other people who are outside of our personal truth who tell us we can't handle it. They aren't usually trying to hurt us (though some may be). They are trying to protect us from getting hurt. They live in a state of fear and look at life from that perspective because it's what they were taught. They don't know how to do things any differently, yet. But YOU do know differently. You know the difference between truth and fear of truth. You know that even if you run from the truth, you still know it for the truth that it is.

That fear of truth – and its consequences – is simply resistance. When we resist, it creates turbulence. When we do not resist, life is smoother.

If you're like most people, you are already resisting that idea. You are thinking there are things you don't like about your life that you must resist. I must resist that cookie. I must resist letting my parents manipulate me. I must resist letting my boss exploit me.

When you try to resist the cookie, it just yells at you louder that you must eat it. When you resist your parent's manipulation, they find other ways of manipulating you. When you resist your boss's exploitation of you, he will find other ways of exploiting you.

Think of the things you do not like as a solid brick wall that is in your way. You can try to push through it, but you'd have to destroy it first. Do you really want to expend all that energy destroying the wall? Does destroying it serve you? Or would it just be easier, more effective, and more conducive to your own peace of mind and happiness if you simply walked around the wall and moved on?

You can create a situation where you don't eat the cookie, aren't manipulated by your parents, and aren't being taken advantage of by your boss **without resistance**.

In other words, instead of resisting (fighting) what is being put in your path, choose another path. It is only your ego that thinks there is only one way to get to where you are going.

REAL LIFE EXAMPLE

When I was having trouble with several clients in my web design business, I was afraid to do anything about it. I was afraid I would lose clients. I was afraid I would lose recommendations. I was afraid I would lose money. I began giving these clients all my free time and energy. It got to the point where I was doing most of the work for free and the business was actually losing money. That means I was paying for the privilege of working for them.

I finally decided I didn't want to be taken advantage of anymore. I wasn't making any money anyway, so I literally had nothing to lose. I started invoicing for the actual work I was doing. I also raised my prices. It was quite a shock for some of the clients to get charged.

It was also quite a shock for me when they not only paid the invoices, but immediately stopped taking advantage of me. The really tough clients simply went away. The only business I lost was business I didn't like or want anyway. The good clients I had been afraid of losing were very happy to pay my new fees because they valued and appreciated the work I did for them. How cool is that!

I didn't resist the abuse I was getting. I simply changed the rules so I couldn't be abused in the first place. Even if the abusive clients stayed, they were being charged a lot of money for the opportunity to be abusive. Once I was actually getting paid what I considered to be a fair wage, I didn't find most of the demands abusive anyway. An interesting change in perception, wouldn't you agree?

I didn't change anyone but myself, and that set of problems disappeared.

Instead of fighting situations I don't like, now I create situations that I do like. Sometimes that means ending a relationship or keeping a safe distance.

I know a woman who spent the majority of her life trying to please her family. Nothing she did was ever good enough. The more she tried to do for them, the more they either ignored her or cut her down. She finally stopped. She didn't turn her back on them or shut them out of her life. She simply stopped trying to do everything for them. That immediately cut the amount of drama by about 75% because, as she discovered, three quarters of the time nobody was asking for her help. It was something she'd put on herself. The other 25% of the time, when they did ask for help, she simply offered a suggestion and then let it go. She accepted that they wouldn't follow the suggestions, so she didn't fight them on it. She answered if asked, and that was it.

It took some time to get out of the habit of jumping in to help, but she finally was able to do it. Of course she still gets saddened when they are in pain, but since they refused to even try her advice, the end result for them is still the same. They never recognized the advice she offered, so they never recognized when she stopped giving it. Because she stopped resisting their refusal to accept help, she has a lot more free time and energy to devote to creating the life she wants to live.

There are plenty of books that go into the esoterics of resistance, so I won't devote a bunch of time to it here. Just remember that "what we resist, persists" and you'll be that much closer to a life filled with more empowerment and less stress.

Inertia

A body at rest stays at rest and a body in motion stays in motion. We humans love our inertia. Once we start moving we hate being stalled, stopped, or rerouted. And once we've stopped, we don't want to move…ever again!

Scenario 1 – In Motion: Have you ever walked up to a door and tried to push it open, only to find out you need to pull? How many times have you actually bumped your nose or chin or twisted your wrist? Have you ever found yourself trying to push it again anyway? As if it's not frustrating enough to have done that, now you have to reverse direction, find the damn handle, get a grip, and pull. The problem, of course, is that you're still standing right up against the door and it keeps banging into your toe!

The only way you are going to get that door open is to get out of the way so it has room to swing open.

Scenario 2 – At Rest: You finally landed that job and it sucks. You spent 6 months in the interview and training process. You have an office, title and a name plate, but you dread going to work every day. The job market is tight and it's just too much trouble to start the whole process over again. Plus, you don't want to see the disdainful looks of your friends and family as you start on yet another job hunt. So you stay.

The reason it's important to be aware of our penchant for inertia is that it, too, is something most of us do unconsciously. Most of the time, we don't realize we're either moving forward or staying still. We are in the thick of things and are committed to our goal.

For the door scenario, it's not that we can't handle the idea of having to pull instead of push. It's that as we approached the door, we already envisioned ourselves on the other side and heading toward wherever it was we were headed. It's an unexpected detour that we didn't factor into our reality.

For the job scenario, we don't want to have to go through the same process we just went through to land the job in the first place.

These things become issues because we are too close to the situations. The guy sitting 15 feet away from the door could have told you it swung inward. He wasn't caught up in your goal so he was far enough away physically and emotionally to have a clear perspective.

Someone who likes their job and didn't just go through the stress of finding one might wonder why you would even think about staying at a job you didn't like.

Going back to cliché references, when you're in the middle of it, you can't see the forest for the trees.

Stress As A Weapon

Being too close to a situation creates stress for you, and it's not only of your own making. If you've ever been in an abusive relationship of any kind, you can probably attest to the fact that the abusers make sure they stay very close to you at all times. If they aren't physically with you, they are contacting you several times a day making sure you feel their presence. They don't want you to be able to get the perspective of either physical or emotional distance because you would then be able to see how much they are hurting you.

Overbearing parents, physically and emotionally abusive partners, employers, playground bullies and even

Madison Avenue marketers use these tactics. They keep the pressure on you as much as they can so you don't have time to think or breathe.

Casinos and amusement parks isolate you and deprive you of any options other than what they have to offer so you feel you have no choice but to play the game their way. Why else would you pay five dollars for a 50 cent hot dog? Why else would you stay in a toxic relationship?

These people and businesses understand how to use stress as a weapon. The government and the news media do the same. They use a steady stream of scare tactics to keep you off balance and unsure and in a state of stress and fear. And when it starts to become too much and the general population begins to resist, they temper things just enough to lull you back into a false sense of security and then start it all over again.

Adapting To The Stress Weapon

Humans, and all living beings, have a remarkable ability to adapt. It is part of our survival instinct. As we have evolved over time, our posture has become more erect, our frontal lobes less pronounced, our teeth smaller and duller. We learned to protect ourselves more effectively from natural dangers, and our bodies adapted.

From an evolutionary perspective, one does not have to consciously decide to develop the tools that are most suited to the environment. It happens automatically. From an empowerment perspective, it's not a bad idea to consciously develop the personal tools that are most suited to the environment.

We are the thinking species. We no longer have to rely solely on our instincts to survive. Before we lived in houses and apartment buildings and structured societies with consciously created laws and processes, it was necessary to have a highly evolved survival instinct. When danger approached, our bodies would release adrenaline so we would have the necessary energy to fight or flee. Developed nations have worked very hard to create environments that are safe from natural dangers. We have developed shelters that protect us from (most of) what Mother Nature throws at us, and laws designed to protect us from what we do to ourselves.

For the people whose highest goal in life is to have power over other people, a problem evolved with all this scientific advancement. They learned that when the overall population isn't afraid, people start thinking for themselves. They become SELF-empowered instead of only having only the power bestowed upon them by those who consider themselves "IN power".

Those people didn't get to be in power, though, because they were stupid. They understood very quickly that as long as the survival instinct didn't atrophy, they could keep the general population scared and tired. The constant rush of fear-based adrenaline wears a person down over time. They can't get enough rest to be at their fullest potential and they remain in a defensive space, trying to protect themselves from a danger that doesn't really exist. This serves the "powers-that-be" very well.

When the majority of people spend their time on the defensive, they shut down their natural instincts. It's ironic that the instinct which protects us is the one that ends up hurting us in the long run. Adrenaline is basically a turbo-boost. It is purposely and properly designed for very short-term use. If you've ever watched a Star Trek film or TV episode, you've seen how staying in warp-drive too long will destroy the engines. Well, that's what happens to us.

Because we are so good at adapting, most of us are stressed out and don't even realize it. The experience of inner peace, true relaxation, is so foreign to us that we feel uncomfortable when we come close to it. We say it is "too quiet". We have come to crave the cloak of noise, discomfort, tension and pain because it is what we are used to.

When we truly relax, we are reconnecting with our true selves. By "true self" I am talking about our spiritual center, soul, and connection to Universe/God/All-That-Is. In more practical terms, it is the recharging of our batteries.

Most of us are living a life that is nowhere near what we really want. My step-sister once said she wouldn't even try lobster because she was afraid she'd like it but would never get a chance to have it again. How have you adapted to life in ways that only result in holding you down?

Personal Responsibility
a.k.a. You Always Have A Choice

Whether you are a passive or aggressive person, it comes from a place of feeling disempowered. The passive person doesn't think they deserve to be empowered, and the aggressive person feels the same way, they just don't want to show it (even to themselves). Again, there is nothing wrong with either one. Don't let anyone tell you that you should be more or less of anything that you are. Just do it consciously.

You ALWAYS have a choice, so choose your battles wisely. Just because someone cuts you off on the highway doesn't mean you have to chase them, and flip them off. But if it makes you feel better, go ahead and do it. Just don't use the excuse that you had no choice. Realize that you are making a conscious choice to take the actions you do.

Nobody makes you do anything. Ever. It's hard to believe, but even as children we were never forced to do anything we didn't want to do. By age 6 (or even earlier) we learned that there were consequences if we didn't do what we were told and (usually, hahaha) made the choice to not suffer those consequences. OK, sometimes we'd be physically forced into the car or pulled away from whatever mischief we were getting into, but even there I've seen lots of children kick and scream and ultimately escape the grasp of many a frustrated parent. It has always been our choice to abide (or not) by the rules and regulations set down by our parents, teachers and other various so-called authority figures. I've known plenty of kids who did whatever they wanted regardless of what they were told to do. If they didn't want to do something, they simply found ways to not do it. They sulked, or cried, or threw temper tantrums. We often judge the people who do these things as being spoiled or obnoxious, but really they are just using the variety of tools they have so they can live the life THEY want to live, not the one the authority figures want them to.

As adults, the most often used excuse for allowing ourselves to be miserable in a job or relationship we hate is that we have no choice. To that I say, "Poppycock!" Even in the worst economic downturn, the classified sections are filled with help wanted and singles ads. New businesses pop up all time by people who recognize a need and try to fill it. Opportunities abound every second of every day for those willing to step even a little bit out of their comfort zones.

I have worked in restaurants, painted houses, done admin work, managed databases, done digital output, graphic design, cleaned houses, data entry, managed a liquor store, worked as an actor, and did the midnight shift at a 7-11. I'm sure I've forgotten a few. I've worked full-time and part-time, long-term and temporary. I've been fired, downsized, laid off, and been eliminated. I've also quit jobs voluntarily.

I've lived in houses, apartments, boarding houses and flea-bag hotels. *(I once saw a cockroach in my New York apartment so big I was able to kill it by hitting it with a stick. I know... ewwwww, right?)* I've been evicted and have snuck out like a thief in the night because I couldn't pay the rent.

I've been jobless and homeless, though thankfully never at the same time.

I readily admit I wasn't always having fun. I worked jobs I hated and lived in conditions I wouldn't wish on anyone. I've been tired of the changes, tired of having to move, tired of changing jobs. But never, not once, was I ever trapped or forced to do anything that I didn't choose, even though it certainly felt that way at times.

If we're going to be honest, you could say I didn't choose to be evicted, fired, or homeless. But, if we're going to be COMPLETELY honest, I have to admit that **it was ALWAYS the choices I made that created the situations I was in**. Sometimes it was due to laziness or lack of motivation. Sometimes it was simple self destruction. Most often it was due to poor decisions based in fear.

No matter what the situation was, there were always choices. Much like political elections, I often didn't like any of the choices that were presented to me, but there were always choices and they were always mine to make.

The moment you blame anyone else for your choices, you are disempowering yourself. Many people put great effort into making others feel disempowered, but when it comes down to it, they can't do anything to you without your consent.

The choices you make are how you wield your power. With this book you now have the tools and the knowledge to live a more powerful life. They say knowledge is power, but if you don't use it, it is worthless. The truth is:

THE <u>APPLICATION</u> OF KNOWLEDGE IS POWER

You are holding knowledge in your hands right now in this book. Don't just read it and expect your life to change. USE the 4 steps. USE the games and tools. APPLY the knowledge.

You are responsible for you.

4 PRACTICAL STEPS TO RADICALLY INCREASE YOUR PERSONAL POWER

STEP 1: BACK OFF

Empowerment is not about fighting or confrontation or heightened negative emotions. But it's really hard to feel empowered when someone is "all up in your grill." (a.k.a. in your face, up your ass, crowding you.) Lots of people tell you to breathe, count to ten, or relax, but if your boss is in your face, your kids are screaming, your partner is freaking out and the guy behind you on the highway is honking and tailgating while the guy in front of you is driving 20 MPH under the speed limit in the passing lane, it's kind of tough to take that breath or count as high as two before wanting to pound someone senseless.

So step one is BACK OFF. This is incredibly easy to do in virtually every situation, yet it's the step we most often forget (or take too far).

So what do I mean by Back Off? I mean literally, physically take a step back.

Have you ever noticed that when a conversation starts to get heated, you move closer to the person? It's often very subtle. We lean in or point our finger. We move into their personal space. It's (usually) an unconscious show of aggression. Even if it's not conscious, we understand instinctively that invading someone's space puts them into a fight or flight reactive mode and that the aggressor, the one who makes that first move, is usually the one with the upper hand. Oftentimes, the other person will be the one who backs down.

This is a very useful tool when used consciously, and one that many aggressive people use for intimidation, but if you aren't aware you are doing it you will most likely alienate and scare a lot of people when that may not have been your intention. Have you ever made someone cringe, cry, or draw away from you when all you (thought you) were doing was calmly and rationally making a point? Have you ever been accused of yelling at someone when you were positive you didn't raise your voice? If yes, then you were probably pushing in without even realizing it.

I used to do it all the time. Especially on the road. Some driver would cut me off, or even just pass me, and it would trigger an angry response. Suddenly I'd find myself tailgating and trying to intimidate the other driver to... what? I don't know. Apologize? Change his ways? Bow down to my perfect driving technique? (My girlfriend is laughing at me so hard right now because contrary to my personal perception of my own brilliance, I'm really not so perfect a driver!)

I'll be honest. I still get angry on the road sometimes. I should probably go into therapy to figure out why I'm so easily triggered there. But regardless of why the emotional reaction happens, I no longer unconsciously use those techniques of aggression that never did anything anyway. Every so often I'll still honk the horn or flash my high-beams at someone, but I know full well that they are empty actions and I usually enjoy a good laugh at myself when I do them.

What do I do instead? I Back Off. Literally. If I find myself driving closer and closer to the person in front of me, I just back off. I allow a little space.

You can do this in any situation when you are in close physical proximity to someone else. Anytime you are with other people face to face: home, office, restaurant, wherever. You can also do it when there are vehicles in play. The only difference is that instead of taking a step back, you would slow down your car a little to allow more space between you and the car in front of you.

This also applies at the supermarket. Another of my pet peeves is getting clipped in the ankles by a shopping cart. Really? Is it seriously necessary to be so close to the person in front of you that you can't keep back far enough to not rip the skin off their ankles?

I've noticed that most drivers don't like to leave too much space in front of them. I think we're afraid someone will cut in front of us. I'm pretty sure this is left over from elementary school when cutting in line was an offense as grievous stealing someone's toy.

Wake up, people. You're not on line when you're driving and nothing bad is going to happen because someone gets to where they're going 10 seconds faster than you do. Why do we drive like we're in a race?

So, yes… Backing Off is not only a great first step in stress relief and empowerment; it is also a very serious, very important public service.

EMOTIONAL RESPONSES TO BACKING OFF

If you are a passive person, you probably back off all the time. It's easier just to let the other guy have his way than to constantly fight and get into confrontations. I'm not talking about backing off to the point of being a door mat. I'm talking about backing off just enough to give you the space to breathe.

Be aware of your own emotional responses. When I was in Junior High School, a gang of bullies surrounded me in the park. They did the typical pushing and shoving and knocking my books to the ground. A high-school boy came by and intervened. While he was taking the other kids to task for being bullies, I quietly picked up my books and walked away.

Whenever I shared this with anyone, whether it was back when I was still a kid, or now as an adult, every person always tells me I did the right thing. You should always walk away from a fight if you can. The problem is that I didn't walk away because it was the right thing to do. I walked away because I was scared and helpless and embarrassed. I was angry with myself for years for being such a coward. In my mind, the only other choice was getting beat up.

Sometimes that old survival instinct comes in handy. My life in that moment may literally have been at stake. If that high school kid hadn't come along there's no telling how the situation may have escalated and I could very well have become another victim of hospitalization or even death from bullying. So from that perspective, it really is fine the way things went down.

The issue is that like most adults, I carried that childhood experience with me and it greatly influenced many of my emotional reactions to situations that didn't even closely resemble that one, but the fear or embarrassment was triggered.

The thing for me to remember now (and you, too), is that I'm not that little kid anymore. I can make my decisions from a place of power, not fear. Even if fear is the primary emotional reaction, I can still make the conscious choice to stay or go, to argue or use reason, to take the high road or the low. In the "if I knew then what I know now" scenario, I would still walk away. The only difference is that I'd do it knowing it's the best choice for me and doing it with a sense of power instead of shame.

If you are a more aggressive person, then backing off is probably a very foreign concept. You will fight to the finish and never let anyone get the better of you. I'll remind you, though, that having power OVER someone is actually disempowering in the long run. That is a very false and short-lived power that you have to constantly fight and struggle to maintain. Every day for you is about confrontation and being right and teaching the other guy a lesson. In other words, it's about pride. Pride is simply the flip-side of shame. So the underlying emotional response to backing off for either the passive or aggressive person is really the same.

Regardless of whether you are more passive or aggressive, Backing Off is not about being a door mat or giving in or giving up. It's about giving you a different perspective on the situation so you can make decisions from a place of power, not fear.

THE RIGHT TOOL FOR THE RIGHT JOB

There are occasions when backing off isn't the best option. Sometimes you have to literally make life and death decisions and don't have time to back off and breathe and weigh your options. Police and fire fighters and paramedics and emergency room doctors often face situations where a split second makes the difference between life and death. But even for them, those instances are the exception, not the rule. More importantly, they have TRAINED for those situations. Our personal experiences can train us for these situations if we pay attention and are willing to learn from them.

Some people use aggressive behavior so effectively that they never give you the chance to back off. If you take a step back, they move in until your back is (literally, sometimes) against the wall. If you find yourself in this type of situation, then you need to take your back off time later. For example, if these episodes happen at work, take time when you are home to think about how different plans of action might be executed. Rehearse in your mind, or with a friend, things you can say or do to diffuse or alter the situation the next time it happens.

REAL LIFE EXAMPLE

I had a woman in a workshop who had a real bully for a boss. He didn't speak TO people, he spoke AT them. He would come in like a freight train, screaming his orders or discontent with the work, and then leave or hang up the phone before any real communication could take place. The woman was in constant fear of losing her job, so she tried to keep her head down and make sure everything she did was perfect. But nothing was ever perfect enough for the boss and she couldn't, from her place of fear, find any way to change things that might not result in making matters worse or even losing her job.

Sometimes you have to think out of the box, and backing off gives the space and time needed to do so. Since we were in the safe space of the workshop and she wasn't in the emotional state of either reeling from the day's assault or dreading going back in, she was open to seeing things from a few different perspectives that I offered.

Most bullies are wounded and scared babies who simply don't know any other way of communicating. They attack so they cannot be attacked. As much as this woman was in fear of being attacked, I suggested that the boss may be in an even greater state of fear made worse by the fact that he didn't know it. Like the lion with a thorn in its foot, he doesn't attack you because he doesn't like you. He attacks because you are near and he is feeling vulnerable.

I suggested to her that she treat the man with overt kindness. I asked her try an experiment. If he yelled at her, she was to ask him if he was feeling all right. Instead of getting defensive, she should show him compassion and sincere caring. Acknowledge that his job is thankless and that it must be difficult to have to oversee so many people who don't appreciate him.

After some discussion about my mental health for suggesting some kind of hippie peace and love compassion for this ogre, she agreed to at least try it once. She couldn't get fired for asking about the man's welfare and showing him kindness, so she was willing to give it a shot.

The simple act of showing him kindness caught the boss so off guard that he forgot to yell at her.

When you back off… i.e. take the time to look at all possibilities of any situation… you can find solutions instead of staying in victim mode.

Steven Covey says "Seek first to understand." Well, you can't do that if you don't breathe, and you can't breathe if you're too close. So get into the habit of backing off and giving yourself the space you need to get perspective on all situations.

THEN ...

DAVID ROSENHAUS

STEP 2: BREATHE

There are few things more aggravating than someone telling you to calm down, relax, or breathe when you're upset about something. We don't want to calm down, dammit, and we shouldn't have to! We have the right to be upset and say so.

ABSOLUTELY!

When we get upset and try to suck it up, bury it down, hide it, ignore it or in any other way not express it, we are actually doing damage to ourselves physically, emotionally, mentally and spiritually. I spent a good portion of my life denying my emotions in general, and my anger in particular. It is truly a medical miracle that I don't have ulcers or high blood pressure. Like many people who hide how they feel, I would often explode over the smallest things or seemingly for no reason at all. It's like a pressure cooker that hasn't let off any steam; it will eventually explode.

I'd always been afraid of expressing my anger. My father shared a story from his childhood when his older brother was wrestling with him and had him pinned down without letting him up. My father went into a panic, overpowered my uncle and slammed his head into the floor so hard it ruptured my uncle's ear drum. He was permanently deaf in that ear the rest of his life.

Because of that, my father rarely showed any emotion whatsoever. He almost never yelled at us, but when he did it was terrifying. I never wanted to be like that so, ironically, I held in my anger also. And I exploded also. Thankfully I've never hurt anyone physically, but I have destroyed a lot of property and many relationships by not knowing how to express or release my intense emotions in a healthy way.

The flip side of that would be a deep descent into depression. Also not a healthy way to express emotions.

So how do you express these emotions in a healthy way? Well, now we're back to calm down, relax and BREATHE.

Our bodies are incredibly intelligent. They know what chemicals to release for which situations. If we eat sugar, a healthy body will release insulin to balance it out. If we are fearful, it will release adrenaline so we can fight or flee effectively. But just like a computer that simply takes the information it is given without discernment to account for human error, our bodies don't know when our minds have made a mistake either.

If you want to know what 2 + 2 is, and you type in 2 + 3, the computer or calculator doesn't know that you MEANT to type 2 + 2. It only knows that you entered 2 + 3 and no matter how many times you yell at it that 2 + 2 equals 4, that calculator will ALWAYS return 5 as the answer.

Our bodies function in the same manner. If you THINK you are under attack, the body will release adrenaline, even if you are perfectly safe. It is your MIND that tells your body the fear exists, and your mind only knows what it PERCEIVES. If your only experience of a dog has been of one that runs at you barking, then leaps up and kisses your face with exuberant love, then you will probably not be fearful if a dog runs at you barking and leaps up to bite you. Until after it happens, that is. From that point on, even if the friendly loving dog comes barking at you, your mind will tell your body it is under attack. Even if you were only bitten once after a lifetime of doggy kisses, your body will always react with fear from that point on (unless you teach it to find a way to process the message of danger in different way like reading YOU to the 10th POWER).

The one thing the body actually gets wrong is the way it handles breathing in the face of fear. Regardless of the situation, our body works much more optimally when breathing is slow and deep, but when fear (real or perceived) is sensed, the body causes our breathing to become fast and shallow. It is only by learning to control our breathing that we can overcome this contradiction and operate optimally when the crap hits the oscillator.

Don't get upset, but this takes time and training. I know, I know... this was supposed to be easy. Sorry, I said SIMPLE. I never said it would be easy. Very little that is worthwhile is ever easy.

But wait! Before you slam the book closed in frustration that I'm asking you to do some work, there is good news. There are a LOT of ways to approach this training and the training itself can be relatively easy if you stick with it.

The key to it all is CONSCIOUS BREATHING. That is, being aware of your breath. It really is very simple. Take a moment right now to be aware of your breathing. Don't change anything. Don't try to breathe a certain way. Just pay attention to your breath right now.

Notice the details...

• Are you breathing through your nose or mouth?

• Are your shoulders rising with each breath, or is your stomach rising?

• Are you breathing deep and slow, or shallow and fast?

• Are you breathing in a steady rhythm or is it more sporadic?

That's all you need to do. Simply pay attention. Do nothing else for right now.

Mastery of any fancy-schmancy breathing technique can only come after you master the awareness of breathing. So for now, don't do anything more. Pay attention to it all day long. It only takes a second each time, but I want you to do it as many times during the day as you can. Try to notice your breathing…

- The moment you wake up
- While you are brushing your teeth
- In the shower
- When you eat
- While talking with
  - a colleague at work
  - your boss
  - your spouse
  - your children
  - your parents
  - your friends
  - your neighbors
  - EVERYONE
- While driving
- While going to the bathroom
- While watching television
- While reading a book
- Etc., etc., etc.

Just keep practicing being aware of your breathing as often as you can. I hope you choose to continue the practice, but for now all I'm asking is that you commit to doing it for the duration of our time together as you read this book.

PUTTING IT TO THE TEST

As the next few days unfold, and you continue to be aware of your breathing in all situations, also pay attention to whether you are seeing changes in your typical day. Do the people around you seem to be acting any differently? Do you notice any change in your behavior or reactions? Again, we're not trying to change anything right now. Simply observe.

My experience with Conscious Breathing is that I become much slower to hit emotional extremes. I'm not so quick to react in anger or go into depression at the usual triggers.

What is your experience with it? I've dedicated a page on my website for people to chronicle their experiences. Feel free to go to *www.DavidRosenhaus.com/You10/experience* if you'd like to share and also see what happened with other people.

HELPFUL BREATHING TOOLS

Don't panic, but I'm going to talk a little bit about yoga and meditation.

Although we're only talking about being conscious of your breathing right now, ultimately the idea is to get you to a place where you have full control over it. Regardless of the situation… whether you are angry, fearful, excited, or horny (no, I'm not being facetious… and I'll discuss it in a little while), you want to be able to control your breathing.

Breath control is essential to self-empowerment. If you can't control your breath, you can't control your emotions. If you can't control your emotions, rest assured other people will control them for you.

There are many ways to learn breath control. Yoga and meditation are two of the more well-known and I've created a list of several others for you that you may want to try at *www.DavidRosenhaus.com/You10/breath*.

I'll be honest. As much as I know I "should", I don't do yoga. I know two positions and occasionally do them as stretches, but as of the writing of this book, I don't practice it (though I really do intend to eventually). With that disclaimer out of the way, I do highly recommend it. At the most basic physical level, it is great exercise and at the highest spiritual level it can help you to connect with your higher self and Source (God, Universal consciousness, etc.).

There are a lot of dissenting views of how yoga should be practiced. Many people would be highly offended that I mentioned exercise in the same sentence because they feel that it is strictly a spiritual practice. I will leave that up to you to decide for yourself. The only reason I mention it is that if you approach certain yoga teachers with the intent of using it as anything less than a direct pathway to higher consciousness, you may get an earful. There are an abundance of classes, schools and teachers out there, so ask questions and find one that resonates with you.

Meditation is something that I actually do practice. I've created a guided meditation for you to get started which you can download from:

www.DavidRosenhaus.com/You10/bathroommeditation.

There are many schools of thought on the "proper" way to meditate. For the purpose of this book, we will define meditation as **complete focus on a single object**. This object can be literal, such as a spot on the wall or a candle flame. It can also be a single word like "love" or a single sound like "om" or a steady drumbeat. Or our breath.

Many people think the purpose of meditation is to clear the mind. This is incomplete, so let's Finish The Sentence *(see page 145)*. The only time the mind is completely clear is when you're dead. I don't recommend striving for that goal. The purpose of meditation (in the context of this book) is to clear the mind... of clutter. This takes practice. Even the most experienced meditaters experience what they call "monkey mind". That chatter-chatter-chatter that happens when things get quiet and you're left alone with your own wacky thoughts. Don't sweat it. It happens to everyone. Even the Dalai Lama.

We live in a society that rejects relaxation. Even so-called couch potatoes watch television or play video games that are designed to excite the nervous system. Even in the escapism of our so-called entertainment we escape our own drama and replace it with someone else's. Truly resting the mind and body is seen as something only for new-age types and Buddhist monks. Although millions of people all over the world play at the game of meditation, it is still not a prevalent part of our mainstream practices. While most of us cleanse our bodies every day (or at least several times a week), very few of us do anything to cleanse our spiritual selves.

I'm a fairly hyperactive guy. My mind goes a million miles a minute and rarely slows down to refuel. Meditation is like refueling to me. Sometimes I'll simply sit and focus on my breathing. In, out, in, out, in, out. It's Conscious Breathing with extreme focus. More than simply being aware of my breath, I focus on it to the point of excluding all other thought. Not that I ever actually achieve it. Extraneous thoughts will always work their way in. With practice, you will learn to simply acknowledge the thought, let it slide past, and refocus on the breathing (or drumbeat, or dot…).

Meditation slows your roll. It trains you to accept a new level of calm into your existence. As with yoga, meditation can be an extremely spiritual practice, but for the purposes of this book, we are using it at its most basic level of the practice of being still in mind and body. You don't even have to wear a sarong or pretzel yourself into the lotus position.

Just sit comfortably, preferably with your back straight. It doesn't matter if it's on the floor or in a chair. I don't recommend sitting on the couch or lying down. It's way too easy to fall asleep (although if you're anything like me, you absolutely WILL fall asleep more than once).

The room should be as quiet as you can make it. Some soft instrumental music is fine. Don't try to soundproof the room. There is no such thing as silence. In 2010 I did a Vision Quest. I was in New Mexico on a mountain at 9000 feet. There were only eight people up there, and when it was Questing time I was far enough away from camp that I couldn't hear them talking. I had very high expectations for the silence up there in nature's perfect hideaway. It never happened. Even a soft breeze rustled the trees. Insects buzzed, birds chirped, and sure enough I could hear the cars driving by from who-knows how many miles away.

So don't worry about the noises. Just don't focus on them. When you hear something, simply acknowledge it, and refocus. When stray thoughts enter your mind, acknowledge them and refocus. When your nose itches, scratch it, then refocus on your object.

The more you practice this, the more you'll see how practical it is in real life. As you train your mind to acknowledge, yet not be disturbed, by distractions, you will find it easier and easier to do in your day to day activities. You'll be able to remain focused on work even while others in the office are chattering or even interrupting you. The boss can come in and have his little freak-out party and you'll be able to acknowledge it, respond professionally, and then get right back to work without it messing up your entire day. Relaxing at home while your spouse and kids are vying for your attention will be much less stressful and taxing on your nerves.

It truly is like magic, but you won't get there just by waving a wand and saying abracadabra. It takes diligent practice to really rock it out.

I would add that with that kind of inner peace comes a natural empowerment that allows you to deal effectively with any situation life throws at you.

Don't get intimidated by the discipline if you are not a naturally disciplined person. Just do the best you can. Just as you did (and are hopefully still doing) with being conscious of your breathing throughout the day, meditate the best you can, when you can.

If you are thinking to yourself that you don't have time, I say you're full of poop. Literally. You have to go to the bathroom sometime. I'm completely serious. After years of trying and failing, I finally got into the habit of meditating by practicing while I was on the bowl. I mean really, what else is there to do while you're sitting there? You can read a book. Maybe you're reading this in the bathroom right now? Take a look at the Bathroom Meditation page 113.

The ability to breathe through any emotion allows you to fully experience the emotion in a healthy way. I used to be the type of person who would bury his emotions in an attempt to control them. That is about as effective as using your bare hands to stop a river from flowing. As any half-baked shrink could tell you, suppressing your emotions does nothing but cause long term suffering.

By processing your feelings and emotions, you can let them go. Therapists' couches (and bank accounts) are filled by people who spent their lives suppressing emotions only to have them resurface years later in any manner of unhealthy ways.

When talking about expressing emotions, many people mistakenly take it as an open invitation to lash out at any perceived slight. That's a bit off the mark. It doesn't serve anyone if you fly off the handle every time you think you've been wronged. It is, however, a really effective way of alienating the people around you and has also been known to be the precipitator of lost jobs and marriages.

What I'm talking about is processing your emotions so you can express them in a healthy way. By practicing Conscious Breathing, I am able to feel (for example) the full extent of my anger in any given situation, yet still remain calm. I can speak the words, "I am angry," without yelling, stamping my feet, or being abusive.

There is a level of controlling it, but not to the point of suppression or holding it in. It is very much like pouring liquid from a pitcher. When we're angry, we often want to dump our entire emotional contents on to the person we are angry at, and sometimes we can't control it. It's like tilting the pitcher too quickly and dumping half the water on the table. The mess just lies there until it gets cleaned up. But when we are conscious... paying full attention in the moment to our breathing and emotions... we will see that we tipped the pitcher too quickly and can adjust it so the spillage is minimal. (Back off) We can then consciously and carefully pour (breathe) the water into the glass, thereby expressing our emotion in a way the other person can easily hear what we're saying without them feeling under attack. The water still gets poured (emotion expressed), but there's no mess. Or at least only a few spilled drops.

So while breathing alone may not sound like such a big deal, the benefits of having full conscious control of it extends to having much better control over our emotions. When we have healthy control of our emotions, we function much more efficiently with much less stress.

This is the essence of personal power, and once we can breathe, it's much easier to use...

STEP 3: CONSCIOUS CHOICE

So we've backed off and taken a breath, now what? In many cases, it won't be necessary to do anything else. In the example of driving, once you've physically backed off and then breathed through the emotional reaction, all the conflict and anxiety and stress is gone. There really is nothing left to do but continue driving to your destination.

Likewise, when dealing with people face to face, a lot of times you'll find that because you handled the situation in such a calm manner, the other person's heightened emotions are also diffused and you can both go on about your business.

Sometimes, though, in the world of interpersonal interaction, things aren't always so simple. Many people get caught in their forward motion. Remember on page 40 (Inertia) when we walked into the door?

It's very possible that no matter how grounded, respectful and peaceful you are, the other person will continue to act as though you are arguing with them or attacking them. Many people's only agenda is to make other people wrong. This can really put you to the test. That's ok. Remember that life is about the journey, not the destination. Just do the best you can in each situation. You are unlearning years of habitual behavior. You're not going to turn into Mother Teresa or Mahatma Gandhi overnight. Or most likely ever. But each time you diffuse or avoid a confrontational situation, it raises your vibration and the vibration of the planet that much more. It also makes life a hell of a lot less stressful and more fun!

Until you've really practiced these techniques, you still may fly off the handle or fall back into depression. You still may botch certain situations. Believe me, I still have my "moments". Just take it as a learning experience and move on. You can back off from yourself, too.

CONSCIOUS CHOICE is where we act like adults. Let's get something straight right off the bat. Being spiritual, empowered, enlightened, or mature does not mean you no longer experience the emotional reaction of wanting to punch someone's lights out or wanting to tell them to just shut the [bleep] up. It means not doing it.

The problem, though, is that there are different WAYS of "not doing it." You can **suppress** your emotions, bite your tongue, hold your temper and then walk away and not say anything. The last time I did that I ended up punching a hole in the wall.

Another more healthy and powerful way of not yelling, screaming and punching is to **process the emotion** by feeling it, recognizing it, and gently releasing it to clear the way for a more rational, safe, productive response. Any response, whether verbal or physical, that attacks the other person (whether they deserve it or not) is not only unproductive, but it hurts everyone involved. You may feel some personal satisfaction in the moment, but the negative feelings will still continue to escalate.

Sometimes yelling may well be the most effective way of communicating in a particular situation. The trick is to make sure you are making the CONSCIOUS CHOICE to yell, for a purpose, and it is not just spewing out of your mouth because it is propelled by your anger or fear or other heightened emotion.

Even if you yell, doing it consciously - by choice - is empowered. You've detached (to the best of your ability in the moment) from the emotional response and you will be able to pay attention to the effectiveness of the choice. You'll be able to tell if you are actually being heard and not just pissing in the wind.

I've found that when I CHOOSE to yell, the other person rarely reacts in the same way as when I used to yell from anger or defensiveness. There is something in the vibration of the conscious yell that the other person recognizes instinctively as being not as dangerous as the anger-propelled yell. Even if they are still in a heightened emotional state, they can feel that you are raising your voice to make a point, and not screaming because you are about to go ballistic.

More often than not, though, when you take that moment to consciously choose how you are going to react, you will end up choosing a more peaceful, solution-oriented form of communication.

If you think that all this thinking is difficult, it might help to realize that you are already doing it. Every time we open our mouths it is preceded by a very complex process of taking in information, comparing it to our past experiences, and deciding on a plan of action. The difference is that the process is driven entirely by the survival instinct that is hard-wired into our bodies. It has nothing to do with long-term relationships, healthy stress levels or peace on earth and goodwill toward man. So CONSCIOUS CHOICE simply brings this process we are already doing into the forefront of our minds.

In the same way we learned to be conscious of our breathing, now we are being conscious of our emotional processing. It takes a little practice, but it's not really too complicated. It also doesn't take very long.

In talking it out, it seems as though there is so much to do. How am I supposed to consider all that input before reacting? It would take 20 minutes to answer a simple question. It only seems like that because words are the most ineffective way of communicating. Our thoughts and feelings are instantaneous, but words take time to think of and say (or write and read).

When you first start practicing your CONSCIOUS CHOICE process, it might take a few seconds longer than usual to do. And those few seconds can sometimes feel like an eternity. Once you get used to it, though, it will flow much more naturally and quickly. Just as when you first learned to drive, you had to take the time to be aware of what your hands were doing and what your feet were doing and looking to the left, right, front and back. Now when you drive, you are still taking all those steps, but you do them in a much more fluid and natural way. Learning to drive your CONSCIOUS CHOICE process is the same thing: a little sporadic and staccato at first, then fluid and smooth.

A great way to practice is to work off-line on recurring situations. What I mean by that is to think about one of those emotionally triggering conversations in your life that you seem to have all the time. Let's say you have a boss who makes you feel small every time he speaks to you. It doesn't matter what the request is, every time he tells you to do something it makes you feel like crap.

Take a moment (like now) to think about these recurring episodes. Go over every detail of it in your mind. Think about the boss:

- What is the expression on his face?

- What is his body language?

- What is his tone of voice?

- What words does he say that trigger the negative reaction in you?

Now let's think about you:

- How do you feel before the boss shows up?

- How do you feel upon seeing him approach?

- How does your body react? (do you shrink back, slump down, put your hands up to protect yourself?)

- Do you get defensive? Aggressive? Tune him out?

- Do you say what comes to mind, or bite your tongue?

Now imagine the conversation differently. It would be nice to imagine the boss treating you better, but we cannot control other people, so let's keep this exercise about what we can control: YOU.

See yourself in your mind's eye going through the conscious choice process. When he barks his order at you, take a moment to identify how you are feeling and why. Is he really saying something offensive or are you just so used to feeling the way you do that you do it automatically every time he opens his mouth (even if it's just to say good morning)? If he is on the attack, is it a personal attack against you, or is he just a generally nasty person? Was he abused as a child? Is he like the lion with a thorn in its foot who doesn't know any better than to scream because he's in pain? Does HIS boss place undue pressure on him, making him feel small and the only way he knows how to overcome that feeling is to pass it on to the next person?

Does your reaction depend on your mood? Is it worse if you haven't had your coffee yet, or do you react in the same way regardless of time or other influences?

Take the time now, while you are in a safe place, to consider all these questions and any others you can think of. We can never really know what drives another person to act the way they do. I'm not making excuses for abusive behavior and I'm certainly not condoning it any way. I am suggesting that we always (to the best of our ability) have compassion for other people because we don't know what their situation is.

The trick is to KEEP ASKING QUESTIONS. Sometimes we are so busy looking for solutions, or hiding from the situation, that we close ourselves off to all the possible scenarios. By asking questions, you keep opening the doors to understanding, even if you never find the "right answer". Simply by being open to the idea that we don't have certain answers, and never will, we open ourselves to having compassion and being able to respect the other person, even if we don't like them or what they are doing.

By reading this book, you now have tools that other people don't. Having compassion for others is a great step in helping you deal with your own emotions because it changes your perception. We often get hurt by other people because we think they are personally attacking us. Even if they ARE personally attacking us, it is often not really personal. It is simply all that person knows in the realm of interpersonal interaction. When you take a moment to consider that they may have personal problems that we have no way of knowing, you begin to see that the attacks probably aren't really personal at the core.

Again, this understanding doesn't excuse or condone their behavior. It simply helps US deal better with OUR emotional stuff and then make choices from a place of love and power instead of fear and weakness.

When we can do that, then NOBODY has any power over us anymore. WE control the situation because we are in control of ourselves.

I have walked away from many relationships because the other person is abusive in some way. Instead of having some big blow-out fight and telling them about themselves, though, I simply allow them to drift away. In the same way I simply stop eating foods I'm allergic to, I just stay away from people who aren't nourishing to my soul.

In the case of a boss or family member, we don't always have the (immediate) option of walking away. So instead, we look at them with compassion. In the same way we might allow a baby certain inappropriate behaviors because they don't know any better, we can't always assume that because a person is physically an adult they have learned more appropriate ways of acting. We only know what WE have been taught and are willing to learn.

Now here's the tricky part... I am NOT saying to suppress your thoughts, feelings, emotions or even judgments. If you get pissed off because you were cut off, so what? You have just as much right to that reaction as the person who cut you off has the right to theirs.

All I'm asking you to do is be CONSCIOUS of your emotions, and make conscious choices about your reactions to those emotions.

Some people get angry and immediately yell, hit, or throw things. They pretend they didn't have a choice. And I say unto you: dingle-poopies! There are very, very few people in very, very few instances who have so little control over their own minds and bodies that they cannot choose their actions.

We say things like, "I couldn't help myself." Really? If a toddler said that, I'd accept it fully, but if you are over the age of 6, you are already choosing your actions. You may not be choosing your emotional reactions, but you are definitely choosing the words that come from your mouth or the physical actions you take.

So let's get back to our boss visualization.

Imagine now what you could change about your reaction. See in your mind how it would look and feel to not shrink back or respond in anger (or whatever your usual reaction is).

Remember, this is only an exercise. Don't think you're required to actually do any of it in real life if you don't want to. You are free to let your imagination run wild. When doing these visualizations, I like to take it to the extreme. Have you ever heard of the technique of a public speaker picturing the audience in their underwear so the idea of speaking is less scary and more fun? Start with that. Imagine your boss in his underwear. Or naked. Or in a pirate outfit. Imagine you have a magic wand and turn him into a toad. Imagine you have fairy dust and when you sprinkle it on him he dances a jig and finally signs off on the raise you were promised two years ago. Have fun with this and let your mind create all sorts of insane and magical situations.

Then bring the focus back to you. Remember, the only thing you can really control is yourself. So in this situation of feeling under attack, if you normally shrink, see yourself standing up tall, chin up, shoulders back knowing he doesn't have the power to change your mood. If you normally get angry, imagine yourself feeling good now that you see his attitude is his problem and not really about you.

When you no longer allow other people to control your emotions (without shutting your emotions off), you are fully empowered. There will always be certain physical things that affect us no matter how much power we have. We can't control traffic. We can't control other people. It is only in knowing, understanding, and having compassion for ourselves and others that we find our power.

Part of the equation is in allowing the other person to be who they are in each moment. So the moment we try to change them in any way, we lose our power.

Try as many different reactions as you can think of. Since it is an exercise, have fun with it. Go ahead and tell the boss where he can shove it. I did this in an exercise once and it was so much fun that the next time the person came at me in attack mode I literally laughed with joy at the memory. I felt a little bad because I was laughing in the person's face. When he asked me what was so damn funny, I told him. Because I was in a joyous mood and only speaking about MY reaction to him instead of talking about what a jerk he was, he not only didn't take offense, but actually saw the humor in the situation. He also began future conversations a lot less confrontationally. My intent wasn't to change his behavior, but because MINE changed, his changed as well. I'll warn you that it does not happen all the time, but in my experience it does happen often.

The key is always to change YOUR actions and reactions, and understand that what the other person does or doesn't do is entirely irrelevant.

As Eleanor Roosevelt said, "No one can make you feel inferior without your permission."

Now that we've learned how to use conscious thought to change how we feel about the situation, let's put it into...

DAVID ROSENHAUS

STEP 4: CONSCIOUS ACTION

As Mahatma Gandhi said, "BE the change you want to see."

So now you've gone through the steps of Backing Off, Breathing, and Conscious Thought. It's time to take action. You've practiced what you'll say to the boss a hundred times now. How you'll show him kindness, compassion and understanding. He'll be so touched by the depth of your caring that he'll never bully or abuse you again. Or maybe you'll stand up and declare how you refuse to be treated poorly and demand to be treated with respect and he'll cry and humble himself and apologize.

Reality check and reminder. You are doing this for you, not for him. You are doing this because this process makes you feel good, not because of any potential outcome. It is in our nature and in our training to do something with a certain goal in mind. That is one of the reasons we so often feel like failures. When we took tests in school it was to get a good grade. For some kids, even an A-minus was equivalent to failure. For those of us who got Cs and Ds it felt as though we would always be losers. It never occurred to us that our inability to make the grade was determined by a number of factors and influences that actually had nothing to do with us. We all learn differently. Some of us are more visual, or aural, or experience-driven. 2+2=4 makes sense to a visual person, but for a person who needs to touch and feel and experience something, it is meaningless. That person needs to touch the two objects and place them next to the other two objects to really understand it.

Most of our failures in learning and applying that knowledge come from a lack of understanding of HOW we learn, not what we're taught. For many of you reading this book, even if everything I said makes sense, you will still put it back on your bookshelf and never take the steps. It's too foreign, or I didn't express it in a way that connected with you. For others, it may just seem too weird or outside the box to work. I really do urge you to take this next step. If you don't put it into action, it will never be real for you, and nothing will change.

The action step is where most of us drop the ball. We think we are going to fail before we even try, so we don't try. Years of perceived failures and false starts and dashed dreams have left us doubtful that we can accomplish anything or change anything. I get it. I've been there. And because I've been there and have still experienced accomplishment and change, I can tell you it doesn't matter what happened in the past. It doesn't matter that you have doubts and fears. It doesn't matter if your parents told you that you would never amount to anything, or your teachers called you stupid, or your friends always made fun of you for not being good enough.

Most of the successful people in the world today started with little or nothing. But they were pissed off enough or driven enough or scared enough of failure to create a reality that was different from what they once knew. It wasn't easy. It took work and dedication and focus. So many of us are afraid of that kind of commitment to success because what if we fail?

Well, what if we SUCCEED? What if, after 20 years of saying I was going to write this book I finally did it? Do I look at myself like a failure because it took 20 years? Or do I look at myself like a success because I actually did it?

The beauty of these techniques is that you literally cannot lose. The biggest risk you face is that some people may look at you funny. It won't make any sense to them.

REAL LIFE EXAMPLE

When I was in my early 20s I planned a trip to Florida. I called all the different airlines to get the best deal (long before the Internet). I was quoted a price $50 less than everyone else and was told to go to my local travel agency to book it.

I sat down with the owner of the agency. He was a big bear of guy and very intimidating. He called the airline and they told him the price I was quoted wasn't valid. He sat up straight in his chair and I thought he would make them an offer they couldn't refuse!

Instead, he very quietly and politely asked for the woman's supervisor. He explained to the supervisor how I'd spent all that time on the phone and how I was quoted this price and even if it wasn't a standard price, they should still give it to me as a sign of good faith. The supervisor said he couldn't do that.

Instead of yelling at him and insisting, the agent said thank you and hung up. He then called a different airline and told them what happened and asked if they would honor the price. No. Supervisor. No. Manager. No.

He called four different airlines. He never got angry. He never threatened or argued or raised his voice. The fifth airline also said they couldn't honor the lower price. However, they could bump me up to first class for the regular coach fare.

This whole process seemed to take hours, but it only took about 20 minutes. I didn't get what I wanted, I got something even better!

I asked him how he could do that without getting pissed off. He told me his Mom had taught him you could catch more flies with honey than vinegar. Here's this huge mook of a guy who could intimidate anyone, and he simply followed the sage advice of a corny cliché he'd learned from his mother.

It was just so weird. So yeah, people might look at you funny when you back off. They might look at you funny when you take a moment to breathe and then consciously choose your words and actions. And though it may confuse and even confound people, your boss can't fire you for being nice. Your spouse can't yell at you because you didn't yell at him. The stranger on the street who bumped into you won't take offense because you smiled instead of lashing out.

So don't let fear of the unknown reaction stop you from taking all four of these steps, especially Conscious Action.

Without putting the steps into action, you will only disempower yourself. Trust me, I speak from experience. The times I've visualized the situation in my mind and prepared to stand up for myself and not be bullied, but then didn't, would emotionally destroy me for days and sometimes weeks. Worse, bullies sense fear. They have even sensed that I was planning to stand up to them and pushed harder.

But just as a bully can sense fear, they can also sense power. I used to get bullied in school every day. One day I had a huge fight with my father before school. As I walked to school, I kept my head down. I tried to look like a victim. I WANTED the usual bullies to come at me. I was pissed and planned to rip the head off any S.O.B. who came near me!

Even though I tried to act small, nobody bothered me that day. Not on the way to school. Not in class. Not after school. Bullies sense power. Even if we try to hide it.

When you are prepared to not be bullied, you won't be. But you have to be honestly willing to take the action. You have to be willing to let the other person be who they are and act how they act without taking it personally (even if it is personal). You have to be willing to ACTIVELY show kindness, compassion, and understanding. You have to be willing to not feel like a victim.

But the key is to actually DO IT. Whether you decide to keep quiet and walk away, show compassion and kindness, or go on the attack doesn't matter. If you go through the conscious thought process of asking questions and being open to the idea of not knowing all the answers and then deciding to do something but don't do it, then you're likely to feel even worse. Going back to thinking about what you woulda-coulda-shoulda said and feeling bad and powerless sucks.

That doesn't mean there won't still be times it happens anyway. This process takes practice. Don't be discouraged if you "chicken out" the first time, or even the first couple of times. Go back to step one and keep working on it until you find a way to take the Conscious Action. Try using some of the games and tools listed in the upcoming chapters to help you get started.

The great thing about this is that the options are endless. There are an unlimited number of responses you can make up and try.

Just remember that it's a game. Hell, whatever you were doing before wasn't working, right? So even if you try something new and it doesn't work, you haven't lost anything. But even if the first 20 things you try don't work to change the other person's behavior, it is working for YOU because now you are taking action. You are no longer a victim. Thomas Edison tried over 1000 experiments before making a light bulb that worked. He didn't stop after the first couple of tries. He knew that he didn't know the answer and that it might take time to find the key.

Keep trying. Keep testing. Keep being in control of YOU. Every time you try something new you grow. And you won't just grow incrementally. You'll grow exponentially. It's a cumulative effect. Every step you take into your own personal power doesn't just add to your power, it MULTIPLIES it.

You have the tools now and there is nothing stopping you from being YOU to the 10th POWER!

DAVID ROSENHAUS

GAMES, TOOLS AND NEW PERSPECTIVES

The following pages are filled with 10 games, tools and new perspectives for you to try on and play with. Whether you believe we live just this one life, or many lives, our time on this earth in this body is limited. You don't know if you will live another 100 years or only a few more hours.

How do you want to live the rest of your life? You could decide right now to start living more fully with less stress and less fear and more power.

Instead of being scared, knowing that our time is limited can be liberating. You have nothing to lose! Of course you can choose to live in a cocoon of misery, but you can also choose to play the game of life with joy and enthusiasm.

Play with these games and tools. Have fun with them. The worse thing that will happen is that you'll start enjoying life more than you ever have.

I'VE GOT A SECRET

One of the first Conscious Action steps I discovered was "I've got a secret". I was still too scared to speak up, even in kindness. But the more I practiced asking questions about things I probably wouldn't ever know – primarily why people act the way they do – the more it sunk in that even if I didn't know why, I knew there WAS a why. I knew it was from their past and had nothing to do with me.

REAL LIFE EXAMPLE

One day I was getting yelled at by my boss and suddenly I started to smile. I suppressed it quickly. I didn't want him to think I was laughing at him. But inside I was jumping up and down. I KNEW A SECRET! I didn't know what the secret was, but I knew he was hiding his pain behind the loud voice and harsh words.

All of a sudden he wasn't intimidating me anymore.

Even though the "action" I took wasn't out loud, it was still actively playing the "I've got a secret" game.

The power he'd had over me immediately lessened and I noticed afterwards that his "attacks" on me were fewer and fewer.

Remember, you don't have to know the secret. You only have to remember that everyone has some big secret they are hiding. That knowledge is YOUR big secret!

BATHROOM MEDITATION

© David Rosenhaus

You can do this meditation anywhere, any time of the day. I call it the Bathroom Meditation because the bathroom is the easiest place to escape to that has the highest chance for you to not be interrupted. Whether you are at work, at home, at a friend's house, or out in a public place, you can always sneak away to the bathroom for a few moments of peace and quiet.

It is very simple, so just read through it once, then close your eyes and do it. You can also download a free mp3 from *www.DavidRosenhaus.com/You10/bathroommeditation* so you can listen as I guide you through it.

> Close your eyes and focus on your breath. As stray thoughts come in, acknowledge them and let them go. Whatever sounds you hear, allow them to fade gently to the background, then put your focus back on your breath. Feel the gentle rhythm of your body as you inhale slowly... and exhale slowly.
>
> Do this for several minutes at least. If you start feeling any discomfort about how much time it is taking, just tell yourself to wait a couple more minutes so you will be able to give your full attention to the things that need to be done.
>
> Return your focus to each inhale... each exhale. Keep breathing until you feel your body relax into it. Feel the stress and tension leave you. Feel the nourishment each breath provides.
>
> Keep breathing. Feel your thoughts relax and your power return, knowing you will now have more energy and clarity to handle the tasks of the day.
>
> Take one last deep inhale, and exhale slowly. Still with your eyes closed, thank your body, mind, and spirit for the support it gives you.
>
> When you are ready, open your eyes slowly. Give yourself a few moments to readjust to the light and your physical surroundings.

If you checked your watch beforehand, and check it now, you will see that you took less than 4 minutes.

This brief meditation will re-center you and allow you to deal with things with a little (or a lot) more ease and grace. No matter where you work, or what your home life is, people will accept going to the bathroom as a legitimate excuse to step out of the room for a few minutes.

Unlike pills, you can take this medicine as many times a day as needed.

Namaste.

THE JOYFUL ALTERNATIVE

What is the joyful alternative? It's so easy to get caught up in right/wrong or good/bad that all we focus on is the problem. If we do focus on a solution it's often the nearest, easiest, fastest thing and it sucks as bad as the original problem. (That's where the phrase "out of the frying pan and into the fire" comes from.)

What if we only chose solutions that made us feel good? Pharmaceutical companies have to produce 60 second commercials for their drugs because 45 of those seconds are filled with all the nasty side effects. Instead of taking drugs, we could choose healthy eating and exercise and loving ourselves. Instead of getting a dozen new ailments from the cure of one ailment, we could be holistically healthy and joyous.

This is just one example of a joyful alternative. Yes, fighting and winning that fight is an alternative, but finding a win/win solution creates joy for everyone involved.

When you try to change a negative situation with a negative solution, you aren't solving anything. You're only exchanging hand-cuffs for chains.

Yes, it takes a little more thought and planning sometimes, but if something isn't working for you, try to find a solution where everyone wins, and no one gets hurt. Find the joyful alternative.

If you'd like to help others by sharing ideas and experiences of Joyful Alternatives you've found, please join the discussion at:

www.DavidRosenhaus.com/You10/experience.

HMMMM... I COULD BE WRONG

I have developed a habit. I call it "Hmmm.... I could be wrong".

This isn't about being morally right or wrong. This is about recognizing that you may not have all the facts, or may have misinterpreted something.

You may be too close to the situation, or not close enough. You may be seeing only one aspect of what's going on but there are many more factors involved.

Even if you've been living with a person for 30 years and think you know their every move, there may still be that one little thing they didn't share with you that affects the situation in a way you never thought possible. How many times have you heard stories of a couple who seemed happily married for 20 years and it suddenly came to light that one of them has been living a double life and has a whole other family in another town? No matter how well you know someone or something, there is always the POSSIBILITY that you don't know everything. Even if you are 100% right, just considering that you COULD be wrong allows you to approach the situation with compassion and patience.

The next time someone cuts in front of you on the highway or at the supermarket, just consider that there may be extenuating circumstances you know nothing about.

Many of us are limited in our choices due to lack of experience. A person who grew up in a house where the parents hit first and asked questions later may not realize there are other options. If you have developed a particular reactionary habit and that has been your go-to response in certain situations, then you are likely to continue doing the same thing.

If this concept is completely new to you it can be as overwhelming as contemplating the expansiveness of the universe. Many people see how huge the world is and they feel small. Some people see how huge the world is and feel they are huge as well because they are a part of it. It's all a matter of perception.

You don't have to know everything. You don't have to be right about everything. You don't have to be right about ANYTHING. As a matter of fact, the minute you stop trying to be right or wrong, your stress levels will drop and your personal power will rise.

Just recognize the truth in all those clichés we've learned to ignore:

1. There are two sides to every situation (actually many more than two).

2. You can't know a person until you've walked a mile in their shoes (you might even try just walking by their side for a couple of miles).

3. Every cloud has a silver lining (or as George Carlin once said: "Inside every silver lining, there's a dark cloud.").

Without some deep and truthful discussion, we can never truly know another person's circumstances. Just because someone is acting like a jerk in this moment, it doesn't mean they are a jerk all the time.

You may not know what pain the other person is in, so when you judge someone (and we all judge…) just remember you could be wrong about them.

> A young child steals a candy bar from a store and we want to punish him – until we find out he's a homeless orphan who hasn't eaten in three days.

> Your own child gets into a fight in school and you are ready to ground him for a month – until you find out he was actually protecting a smaller kid from a bully.

> You get stood up on a date and are feeling hurt and dejected – until you find out your date was in an accident and spent the night unconscious in the hospital. *(Yeah… I stole that one from a movie, but it's a really good example.)*

The facts of each of these situations didn't change. Only your perception of them did. And your perception changed **based on your knowledge and judgments of the facts**.

IT'S YOUR CHOICE (THE PISTOL PARABLE)

We fear the unknown even if we are pretty damn sure it's a better place than where we are now. We love to play the "hmmm… I could be wrong" game with things that might benefit us, but assume we are always right when we think something is bad.

In other words, **we purposely choose not to find a different perspective**.

It's very easy to blame others for pushing in and applying pressure. We THINK we are victims of other people's actions, but that is simply not true. Even though we don't always know how, if we are adults, we ALWAYS participate in what happens to us.

While there are certainly very real pressures put on us by family, friends, society, and many others who thrive on having power over others, there is not a single pressure that an adult human being doesn't consent to giving in to.

Many of us love to use the excuse that someone "put a gun to my head". First of all, I'd venture to say that more than 99.9% of the time it's probably an exaggeration. But let's take it at face value and assume for a moment that someone is actually holding a very real gun to your head and telling you to do something.

YOU DON'T HAVE TO DO IT!!!! It is still a choice.

The first thing you do with that gun to your head is ASSUME you only have two choices: live or die, and that death is not an option. It is part of our conditioning that everything that happens to us needs to be a life or death situation. Understand that you have many more possibilities with a gun to your head than life or death. Let's take a moment to look at a couple of them, starting with the things we do not, and cannot possibly, know.

Before the trigger is pulled, we do not know:

- if the gun is loaded

- if the safety is off

- if the gun has been properly maintained and actually works

- if the gunman will actually pull the trigger

After the trigger is pulled, we do not know:

- if the gun will misfire

- if the bullet will ricochet off the skull and not kill us

- if the bullet will miss us due to the trembling hands of the gunman

- if the bullet will go straight through our head without actually doing damage

All of these things have happened in real life. And those examples are only the ones assuming we take no action of our own. What if we tried to:

- Run?

- Talk our way out?

- Duck?

- Fight?

Even in this extreme but real scenario of an actual gun at our heads, I have shown you several possibilities that aren't usually taken into account when we limit ourselves to only having live or die as the possible outcomes.

I have offered you several actionable options other than giving in to the demands of the person holding the gun. I'm sure there are others my limited imagination hasn't considered. If you think of more, post them in the forum at *www.DavidRosenhaus.com/You10/experience.*

The point of this is that you ALWAYS have options. Maybe those options suck, but you always have options. The sad thing is that most of us will choose the option that is EASIEST, not the one that is OPTIMAL.

Which will you choose?

PLEASE DON'T EAT THE EMOTIONAL GARBAGE

On an emotional level, Steven Covey calls nourishment your emotional bank account. As with our financial bank accounts, most of us don't like taking risks because it's... well... risky. We protect ourselves from physical, emotional and mental pain by playing it safe. If we ask "what if?" and any of the possible answers involve pain or discomfort, most of us won't do it.

Where does that get us, though? Let's look at some of your personal experiences to answer that question. Have you ever:

- Stayed in a relationship long after it was over because you didn't want to hurt someone's feelings?

- Stayed in a relationship long after it was over because you just didn't want to be alone?

- Stayed in an emotionally or physically abusive relationship longer than 2 instances of abuse?

- Stayed in a job that made you miserable?

- Stayed in a job where there was no chance of advancement or growth?

The two driving forces in most people's lives are love and money. We can't live without either one and we would rather eat garbage than go hungry.

There is nothing empowered about eating emotional garbage. But we do live in a world with other people, and... if we want to get along in a positive social environment... there will always be compromise.

Sadly, many people don't know the difference between compromise and garbage. For those of you who are the sensitive, giving types like I am:

Emotional garbage is what doesn't add to your emotional bank account. For example, doing what someone asks without question and never asking for, or receiving, ENOUGH in return.

What is ENOUGH? Enough is what you need to keep going in a healthy manner. Not everyone needs three gourmet meals a day to stay healthy. Some people feel great with two small balanced meals, and others feel awesome having small snacks throughout the day. But EVERYONE has to eat SOMETHING.

If you are constantly doing things for others without anyone (including you) doing something for you, it emotionally depletes your bank account. Many of us "givers" tell ourselves that our reward is being in service. This is true up to a point, but it doesn't hold up in the extreme or for the long term. Just as with a financial bank account that pays interest of less than 1% while inflation is 4 or 5%, if you don't make substantial deposits regularly, your balance will eventually disappear.

Sometimes we do something for someone and they smile. That is nourishment and can keep us giving forever. But if we are in a relationship where we give and never receive acknowledgement, reciprocation, or any indication that what we've done is appreciated, it will destroy us. It may take 20 or 30 years, but eventually our batteries will run down and we break down.

We are so good at adapting and the decline of our emotional, physical, and spiritual health is so slow that we can easily fool ourselves into thinking it isn't happening.

This is what we are doing with our planet. Pollution, the depleted ozone layer, the escalation in the variety and strength of viruses and diseases are all obvious signs that we are emptying the Earth's bank account. But because the death tolls aren't rising fast enough to scare the crap out of everyone, most people choose to ignore it.

It is the same for one-sided relationships. We tell ourselves we are strong enough to handle it. We tell ourselves that our partner or boss or parent or child will one day appreciate us. We tell ourselves we are the only person in the world who can save them.

And slowly, but surely, we are killing ourselves.

It can be argued that we're all gonna die one day anyway, and isn't it oh so noble to be a giver, even if nobody appreciates it. That is a great argument for someone who is unworthy of love.

Let me set the record straight for you. There is not a single person in the entire universe that is unworthy of love. Religions and individuals who want power over people are the only ones who will ever tell you that you are unworthy of love. They are wrong. They tell you this so they can control you.

Do you get it? Are you finally listening? It doesn't matter what so-called "sins" you've committed, or on what side of the tracks you were born. Every single person deserves to be loved. Every single person is powerful in their own way.

Every person is just as worthy as every other person. Including you. Period!

So stop giving away your power.

Stop emptying your emotional, spiritual and physical bank accounts.

Stop eating emotional garbage.

Right now!

POSSIBLE COLORED GLASSES

Having power OVER others does not make you powerful. Real power comes from within. Real power is the ability to be happy right where you are in each moment no matter what the circumstances. Real power is not allowing others to have power over you.

This is not achieved by having power over them. It is not achieved by fighting. It is simply not allowing anyone to change who you truly are. "They" can take your house, car, clothes and all possessions because they are physically stronger. They can NOT take YOU. The person you are. The love you are. The divine and infinite being you are.

Nelson Mandela spent 27 years in jail and never lost his power. That is why he was able to come out and become president of the nation that imprisoned him.

Viktor Frankl spent 3 years in a Nazi concentration camp and went on to become a leader in the psychotherapy field and wrote a book about his experience using his method of finding meaning in all forms of existence and thereby having a reason to continue living.

These people may be exceptions to the rules we know, but only because we know the wrong rules. In your heart, regardless of your experiences, you know that you are an infinite being. You know that you are all-powerful.

What you may not know is that it is not in the physical world that you are infinite and all-powerful. It is as a spiritual being. The trouble we have is because we live in a physical world.

Here's the kicker... we are in this physical world to give ourselves a different perspective from which to experience that power. How many times have you mastered something and then challenged yourself to go bigger, better, faster?

If we aren't challenged, we get bored. That is part of being an infinite being. We want to push the limits, but as a spiritual, ethereal being, there are no limits. So we create realities which put us into limiting circumstances so we can have the joy of getting past them.

In the athletic event of the High Jump, Dick Fosbury changed the world. Prior to 1968, the record for the high jump was 7'5¾". Fosbury used a completely different technique and literally raised the bar. Since then, the unsurpassable height of seven and a half feet has been exceeded as the norm and the new record is 8 feet!

Fosbury simply did it differently. He saw the possibilities and looked at the challenge from a different perspective. The few people in the world who control most of the money and power aren't any smarter or stronger than the rest of us. They simply do and see things differently.

They are willing to break out of the "norm" and recognize that what doesn't work for them must be changed. They act as infinite beings.

If you're like me, the phrase "infinite being" may not really have a lot of meaning. It wasn't really in the realm of my understanding in this physical world.

Try this phrase on for size: "The POSSIBILITIES are infinite."

How does that feel? A little uncomfortable maybe? But still, something that you might be able to get a grasp on, right? It doesn't say you WILL achieve anything. It simply says that it's POSSIBLE.

Here's the catch. When you start looking at the world through possible colored glasses, there are certain words you can no longer use. Like "can't".

You can no longer say it can't be done. You must take personal responsibility and ownership that you choose not to do it, not that you can't. Maybe you tried and failed, but that only means you didn't do it YET.

YES, AND...

"All the world's a stage, And all the men and women merely players."   *William Shakespeare*

Believe it or not, you can learn a lot about empowerment by doing the work of an actor. OK, don't stress out... I'm not suggesting you get on stage.

The biggest difference between an actor creating a character and a person in real life is that actors know they are the creator. Yes, they've been given limitations, but they still have choices. They have to say the specific words written in the script, but they choose HOW they're going to say them. They have to do certain actions that the director gives them, but they choose HOW they're going to do them.

Another way in which real life correlates to an actor's life is that even though we have a script, the really important stuff is usually revealed when something happens that deviates from that script. Most of us grew up with certain expectations about how our lives were going to go. And for most of us, it didn't work out that way. That's exactly what happens when creating a character.

One of the ways an actor prepares for these deviations from the script is called Improvisation or Improv, for short[2].

Many actors are afraid of Improv. Many regular folk are, too. The script is like a security blanket and the thought of thinking for your self can be terrifying. (Hmm… just like life.) Once they get a handle on it, though, it frees them to create a whole new character and discover things far beyond the boundaries of the script. (Hmm…just like life.)

The core of improvisation is "Yes, And…"

---

[2] Improv is acting without a script, or ad-libbing. If you aren't familiar with it, look up "Whose Line Is It, Anyway?" This is a TV series in both the UK and US where they play improvisational games.

The most important rule of Yes, And… is never deny.

For example, if someone looks at you and says, "You're from the planet Concocta," you do not say, "There's no such place." That would end the scene abruptly, and the audience would get ripped off.

Instead you say (something like), "Yes, I am from Concocta **and…** I'm here to take over your planet." Now the scene gets interesting.

You may be wondering what any of this has to do with living a stress-free, empowered life. Well, I'll tell you.

Living your life by the Yes, And… principal frees you from the confines of your mental, emotional, spiritual and even physical prison.

When you embrace everything instead of resisting it, you have found your personal freedom. When you begin each and every reaction with Yes, And… you'll find that a huge weight lifts off your shoulders.

If someone is doing something you hate and your first response is Yes, And… you are forced to find a proactive solution from a place of empowerment… forward action… instead of a place of stuck resistance.

When you resist something you are holding your ground. That means digging in your heels and not moving. You can never move forward from a place of resistance. The minute you try to stop someone from doing something you are stopping yourself at the same time. Remember, resistance is futile.

For example, in many martial arts you use the movement of the attack to throw the attacker off balance. You don't try to stop them. You let them do what they are doing and then respond in a way so their actions become ineffective.

When you try to stop someone from doing something, they will only try harder. The only way you can stop them is to overpower them. Now you are exercising power over someone else and taking away their free will. We never want someone doing that to us, yet we often try to do it to someone else.

> *"I was once asked why I don't participate in anti-war demonstrations. I said that I will never do that, but as soon as you have a pro-peace rally, I'll be there."*
> Mother Teresa

Mother Teresa understood that you empower yourself by creating instead of fighting or destroying.

Let's say you are in a bad relationship. Your partner treats you horribly and you want it to stop. You plead and you argue, but the abuse continues. You cry and you scream and you lock yourself in your room, but still it continues. You fight back, but become exhausted, and still it continues.

Finally, you say Yes, And…

Now what? Let's break it down. Saying yes is not condoning your partner's abuse. It is recognizing, accepting and acknowledging that it is happening. That it is real. That it is how he has chosen to exercise his free will.

And…? Now you must make conscious choices. That means taking action instead of only reacting. You have tried reason. You have tried begging. You have tried crying. You have tried everything you could think of to change the situation by changing the other person. Now it is time to change the situation by changing your actions.

Excuses:

- But I love him/her!

- But I need the job!

OK, so stay. But stop complaining. You have made your choice. If the price of being abused is cheaper than the price of leaving, that is your choice. Stop feeling sorry for yourself and accept (YES) that this is your choice and that you made it consciously. Accept (YES) the other person for who they are and how you have **chosen** to allow yourself to be treated.

Yes, I am being abused, And... I love the person or feel that I need the job enough to continue accepting that behavior.

Some people may look at that choice and think it is disempowered, but as long as you have made a CONSCIOUS choice, you have made an EMPOWERED choice.

However, the minute you do anything because you think you didn't HAVE a choice, you are coming from a place of disempowerment. You are also mistaken.

You always have a choice. Non-action is a choice. Taking abuse is a choice. Living with anything that goes against what you believe is a choice.

Remember though that those are not WRONG choices. There is no right or wrong, there is only what is.

Practicing Yes, And... completely changes your perspective on things. If you play it with full commitment you will find that you are never stuck. You are always actively engaged in the creation of your life. By saying "yes" you are not necessarily agreeing with anything. You are simply accepting that the situation is what the situation is. Adding the "and..." allows you to increase the joy or change the direction of the pain. "No" limits you. "Yes" frees you.

Life will always continue moving forward whether you want it to or not. It is up to you whether you will or won't actively participate in the direction the movement is heading.

FINISH THE SENTENCE

This is one of the most powerful, perspective-changing tools you can have in your empowerment tool belt.

Thomas Edison failed over a thousand times before making a light bulb that actually worked the way he wanted it to. Let's take special note of the end of that sentence. "The way he wanted it to." That sentence could have ended with him failing "over a thousand times before making a light bulb that actually worked PERIOD". That wouldn't be true, though. Many of the "failed" bulbs worked. Some worked for a second. Others worked for a couple of minutes. They worked, just not the way Edison wanted.

How many things in your life are working, just not the way you want them to? Do you just give up then and end the sentence with "it doesn't work"? Or do you finish the sentence with "the way I want it to"?

If you add that little coda ("the way I want it to") to the things you don't like or aren't working in your life, it opens the door to the infinite possibilities. Yes.... and....

If you are trying to open a package that has 4 pieces of packing tape on it, but only remove three of them, the box won't open. That doesn't mean that removing the tape doesn't work. It means that removing 3 out of 4 pieces of tape doesn't work. Sometimes that package has several layers of tape. (Don'tcha just love that? Somebody triple wraps the box like it's hazardous waste material instead of a birthday gift and you have to break out the circular saw to open the darn thing. But I digress...) Inconvenient, yes. Impossible, no.

THERE IS NOTHING THAT IS IMPOSSIBLE.

There are only things we haven't figured out yet.

How easily are you willing to give up? Decide that first, then Finish The Sentence.

KILL 'EM WITH KINDNESS

Another great tool I discovered by accident is "kill 'em with kindness". As mentioned in the real life example in the BACK OFF chapter, showing kindness to a unkind person can result in a change in their attitude. Even if it doesn't, you will feel better about yourself for not having backed down and shriveled up. You will have taken action in the face of the other person's attack and not played the victim.

A lot of people think I'm just being all la-de-da when suggesting this tool, but as you'll soon see it's a really strong offensive tactic.

REAL LIFE EXAMPLE

One of my earliest jobs was working in restaurants. I was the lead waiter at a family restaurant so when the other servers had issues, they would come to me first before going to a manager.

During one busy dinner rush, a waitress came to me crying because of an abusive customer. I went to the man, who not surprisingly was eating alone, and asked what the issue was. He rudely expressed his dissatisfaction with the service he'd been getting. I told him I would take care of him and see to it that he was properly taken care of.

This man was one of the rudest and meanest people I've ever met in my life. It became clear very quickly that his sole purpose in life was to make the people he came in contact with as miserable as he was. He complained about every detail of the food, the service, the restaurant, the other customers, and even the décor.

I made sure his food was prepared exactly as he ordered it, but he would still complain that the order was wrong and send it back. To give you only one example, when he ordered dessert he ordered a slice of apple pie. When I brought it to him he complained it wasn't warm. When I brought the warmed pie to him he complained that it wasn't ala mode (which he didn't ask for).

Now here's the fun part. The more he complained, the more I smiled. The more he lied about his order being wrong, the more I said "yes, sir, I'll take care of that right away".

What I did NOT do was apologize. No matter how many time he accused me of being incompetent and even stupid, I never once apologized. I would only tell him that I would take care of the problem and get him what he wants.

The nicer I was to him, without *ever* apologizing or making myself small or wrong in any way, the madder he got. You know how red Elmer Fudd would get when Bugs Bunny outsmarted him? This man literally got Elmer Fudd red.

By the time he got the bill, I seriously thought he was going to have an aneurism.

So when I suggest that you be nice to people who are mean, it's really not only some la-de-da fru-fru kumbaya thing. If the best defense is a strong offense, then kindness fits the bill more often than not. It not only disarms the other person because they soon realize they can't control you, but it also puts you on the higher moral ground.

It's always satisfying when we lose our temper and our friends and supporters tell us we had every right to. It's even *more* satisfying when even your enemies and detractors are virtually forced to take your side because you didn't sink to the other person's level. The worse thing they could accuse you of is faking it. But they can't bring you into the mud and say you're as bad as the other guy because you fought back or lost your temper.

CONCLUSION

Part of the process of standing in your own power is recognizing that you already have it. We all have doubts about ourselves. We all wonder if we're good enough, how we fit in, and what contribution we can be to the world. While developing this system, I realized that most people already do much of what's written here. Although I approach it from my unique perspective, very little of it is new information.

I'm reminded of this every time I teach a workshop. So many participants share how they have already been putting most of these techniques to use. So I questioned why it was working for me, but not others. What I realized is that the key difference is in the CONSCIOUS application of the tools.

We instinctively BACK OFF. We instinctively BREATHE. We think and take action all the time.

If we are not fully conscious of the process, though, we become slaves to our instinct instead of masters of it. We allow ourselves to be ruled by emotion and habit, and then wonder why things don't change.

When you make your choices consciously, you are empowered. It's not about right and wrong, but about learning what works - for you. If you feel stuck in a situation, then ask yourself if you really, truly want to get unstuck. What choices are you making that keep you there? What habits do you refuse to break that won't allow you to move on?

If you step back and really see what's going on, you will find that you are always successful at achieving the things that are supported by your actions. Unfortunately, those things are often not what we really want. Only by changing your actions can you change the outcome.

Many people stay in abusive relationships because their beliefs about loyalty and commitment are stronger than their beliefs about abuse. Others stay because their fear of the negative consequences are stronger than their confidence in their ability to change things for the better. That's OK.

There is absolutely nothing wrong with you if you choose to not make any changes in your life. The only important thing is that you realize, recognize and accept that it is YOUR choice.

Don't use duty or loyalty or religion as an excuse to be miserable. If, for example, your commitment to marriage is so complete that you choose to stay married even if there is physical or emotional abuse, infidelity, or any other challenges, then be happy with your choice. Stand proud and strong in knowing that you are honoring your beliefs.

You are not a martyr. You have consciously chosen your situation. Many people enjoy the "poor, poor me" song. They enjoy the attention they get from people who feel sorry or commiserate with them. There are very often great rewards for playing the victim. If those rewards are what you want, then by all means continue as you were. Just don't pretend that you have no choice in the matter. You ALWAYS have a choice.

As the consciousness of the earth's people continues to grow, the sympathy card will be less and less effective. People will stop feeling sorry for others who make choices that put them into bad situations.

One example of this is the people who live in the area of Malibu, CA. They face mudslides and fires every year. Every year when the fires or floods hit, there is shock that it happened. Every year in that region someone loses all their possessions and memories and cry because they were victimized by Mother Nature. They pretend that there was no fire or mudslide the year before, and the year before that, and the year before that.

Is that how you view your situation? Do you keep having the same experiences in your life over and over and then when it causes severe or irreparable damage you are surprised?

I often wonder why people feel the need to wait until their lives are destroyed before they make changes, but more importantly I wonder why they always act astonished that it happened.

Whether you make changes or not, you are now choosing consciously. You can no longer pretend you don't know any better. If you choose to remain in the same situation, job, or relationship that is causing you pain, be secure in the knowledge that you chose it.

You are not a victim. You are not helpless. You are a conscious being making choices every moment of the day. If you don't like the outcome of those choices you have the power to change those choices.

The *conscious you* decides what action or non-action you will take next. The *conscious you* realizes that every moment is only an experiment in cause and effect. The *conscious you* knows that life is a game in which you make the rules.

The *conscious you* is YOU TO THE 10th POWER!

ACKNOWLEDGMENTS

This book is a product of a lifetime of experiences. It would not exist without every person who ever laughed at, yelled at, scorned, shunned, hated, rejected, schemed against, undermined, refused, abused, confused, used and put me down.

It also would not have happened without incredible thought leaders like Tony Robbins and Louise Hay and all the authors, speakers and teachers who share their passion for the expansion of our minds and souls.

I humbly thank and honor each and every person who came into my life and gave me the opportunity to grow.

ABOUT THE AUTHOR

David Rosenhaus is an author, speaker, empowerment specialist, and spiritual mentor. He guides you through life's challenges with charisma, compassion, creativity, and a healthy dose of humor. David's unique career path (including stints in graphic and web design, entertainment, the restaurant business, theatrical coaching, the corporate world and more...) has given him a broad range of experiences along with an encompassing perspective. It's this perspective that allows him to work with people on a very practical, effective level.

David is passionate about teaching people that they each have something positive to contribute to the world, that they do not have to accept being treated like doormats, and that everyone has the power to choose. His dedication to contributing positive changes in perception and spirituality around the world has a broad appeal to both men and women.

David's innate ability to simplify the complicated has led him to create the You to the 10th Power Empowerment System. The You10™ System gives you the same tools David employs himself to find relief from the mental habits of stress and depression - opening the door to a life free from fear and limitations.

David has also created the Rock and Roll Oracle™ Empowerment Card Deck, which allows the user to tap into and develop his or her own personal spiritual energy. Using the Rock and Roll Oracle cards will help provide the guidance you've been seeking to make practical, lasting changes in your life, not to mention rekindling the love of this magical musical genre.

David is available for personal Rock and Roll Oracle™ readings, YOU10™ workshops, speaking engagements, and personal coaching sessions.

NOTES

NOTES

www.ingramcontent.com/pod-product-compliance
Lightning Source LLC
La Vergne TN
LVHW011233080426
835509LV00005B/474